Fashion Installation

Fashion Installation

Body, Space, and Performance

ADAM GECZY and
VICKI KARAMINAS

BLOOMSBURY VISUAL ARTS
LONDON · NEW YORK · OXFORD · NEW DELHI · SYDNEY

BLOOMSBURY VISUAL ARTS
Bloomsbury Publishing Plc
50 Bedford Square, London, WC1B 3DP, UK
1385 Broadway, New York, NY 10018, USA

BLOOMSBURY, BLOOMSBURY VISUAL ARTS and the Diana logo are trademarks of
Bloomsbury Publishing Plc

First published in Great Britain 2019

Cover design by Philippa Thomas
Cover image: Aitor Throup show during The London Collections Men SS17 on June 12, 2016 in
London, England. (© Victor VIRGILE/Gamma-Rapho/Getty Images)

A catalogue record for this book is available from the British Library.

A catalog record for this book is available from the Library of Congress.

ISBN: HB: 978-1-350-03251-4
       PB: 978-1-350-03252-1
       ePDF: 978-1-350-03250-7
       eBook: 978-1-350-03253-8

Typeset by RefineCatch Limited, Bungay, Suffolk

To find out more about our authors and books visit www.bloomsbury.com
and sign up for our newsletters.

CONTENTS

ILLUSTRATIONS

INTRODUCTION
INSTALLING FASHION

As the term is conventionally used in contemporary art, "installation" refers to a form that uses, or occupies, space. The space can be the architectural space of the gallery or museum, or the architectonic siting can be more imaginary and transient, such as when a work of art occupies areas outside of conventional exhibition spaces. Another way of thinking of installation is as a rejection of the "plinth" attitude to the object, where the plinth or frame suggests an ideal or decontextualized way of understanding. In other words, the plinth requests that the viewer discount all the external values that encircle the object and see the object only in and for itself. By contrast, installation asks that these very qualities are essential to the way the object is understood. As such, installation is an approach that is material and immaterial, in the sense that it rejects any possibility that a work of art can be viewed objectively, or in isolation of space, time, culture, or history. The role of the body becomes very important in this dynamic, both in terms of the viewer in the space of the installation, or any other bodies that serve as components to the overall work. According to this definition, "installation," as it has come to be known in art, is aptly suited to the ways in which fashion is presented and displayed, and increasingly, over the last twenty years, when designers have availed themselves of more and more sophisticated systems by which to convey the fashion object, which exists not in isolation but across a network of representations and narrative connotations.[1]

The need to explore this term is prompted, among other things, by the very unease with which the term "catwalk" is used today. For "catwalk" is used more metonymically than literally, to refer to the *mise en scène*, the staging and launch of a particular collection, as opposed to the traditional catwalk as such. Indeed, the catwalk is and was the equivalent of the plinth for a work of sculpture, or the frame for a painting, print, or drawing, namely a divider that then implies a neutral space in which the object is seen and understood. The mythology of an ideal and objective way of looking at an object is as convenient as it is coherent, as it does not differentiate between the myriad mitigating factors that generate meaning. While no work of art (or fashion) claims to be autonomous, the consciousness that it is installed entails an acknowledgment of the constituents that comprise the meaning of a thing.

The difference between the rationalized and objective framing of fashion is best exemplified by the beginnings of fashion display. Evidence dating back to the end of the fourteenth century tells us that the most popular form of circulating and communicating trends in clothing and dress was through dolls. In 1515, François I requested dolls to be made after the clothing worn by Isabella d'Este, so as to instruct the ladies of his court about what to wear.[2] But there is nothing to suggest that the dolls were necessarily in her likeness; rather, they were simple armatures for the sake of expediting a particular goal, which was to ensure that François's court was commensurately elegant as befitting of his own majesty. With the birth of couture in the latter decades of the nineteenth century, Worth made use of living models to show off his creations, but the generic name for models was *mannequin*, a term still in use today, despite being destabilized by the celebrity model and the supermodel, who were anything but generic. Another French term in use for models was *sosie*, or double, ensuring that the model be treated as a cipher subordinate to the clothing she carried on her back. Fashion illustration and photography of the turn of the century also maintained a relatively clear division between items of fashion and other extenuating terms of reference. Generic figures were either placed in isolation or in void against the page or plate, or otherwise would be placed against an innocuous background of decoration or of the activity to which the garment related.

The first stage in the lineage we attempt to trace—a genealogy using the lens of the notion of installation—arrives with Edward Steichen's series of images in 1911 for a collection by Poiret. These photographs were as a result of a challenge by the editor of *Gazette de Bon Ton* and *Jardin des Modes*, Lucien Vogel, to raise the stakes of photography and to lift it to the status of art. For this series, Steichen departed from the stark figure–ground convention of fashion photography and placed the models *within* a setting, and posing in a manner that favored transitional movement over stasis, thereby conveying a sense of narrative. The only precedent to this were the so-called "fashion plays" popular in France and England in the 1890s, in which the skeleton of some plot was used as the excuse for showing off fashion items. From then on, fashion and the theater would continue to have a close and interweaving relationship.[3] Seen as imbibed by drama, body and clothing assumed a diegetic character. The clothing that the models wore was intended to be read as a component of space and time, existing within a set of codes and intentions that well exceeded what the immediate image portended. But before delving deeper into these relationships, it is worth considering some of the fundamental aspects of installation practice as they evolved in art.

Art and installation

In contemporary art, there is a widespread assumption that all art is to some degree installed, irrespective of whether the art is deemed installation or not. This is based on the assumption that no artist or curator takes for granted the conditions by which a work of art is seen. These considerations may be minimal, such as taking into account an architectural feature such as a door or a window in the placement of a painting, or they may be highly consequential, as with site-specific work, where the object(s) are meaningful only according to where they are placed. Installation, then, is as much a state of mind as it is a practice. For example, to see a painting by Van Gogh in Arles is a different experience from seeing the same painting in a museum in Tokyo. For to see it in Arles is to have the work imbued with the history of the painter's time there, while to see it in Tokyo is to have the work colored by a particular history of the 1980s when the Japanese bought works by this artist for record prices as an assurance of their European humanist cultural affinities. On a completely different scale and with different intent, in Michael Asher's 1970 work *Installation*, the gallery of Pomona College in California was reconfigured and left open for twenty-four hours of the day, exposing it to all the goings-on outside, including all the external noise and detritus. Much as, in the manner John Cage conceived of music as the sounds that occurred when a musician did not play, Asher's "work" was to lay the conditions for what occurred. The reconfiguration of the gallery space was not to be considered in and for itself, but rather as the stage upon which the subsequent random elements played. Asher was an important artist working within an installation genre known as "institutional critique," whereby artists did not create things to be placed in museum and gallery spaces, so much as organize problems and resituate existing objects to beg questions about the role, history, and mission of the space itself.

By this account, installation art is inseparable from conceptual art. It is one of the prevailing misconceptions of the art of the last forty or so years to separate the various "isms" in the way that could be conveniently done by the movements of the late nineteenth- and twentieth-century avant-garde. Movements such as Cubism, Orphism, Futurism, Constructivism, and so on, while often sharing formal qualities and occasionally members, all had fairly coherent sets of attributes and followed quite specific trajectories which, in retrospect, could be historically circumscribed. By contrast, the various tendencies (rather than movements) from the 1960s onward—Art&Language, land art, conceptual art, performance art, happenings—all arose from shared interests in divesting art from the tyranny of the commodifiable, fetishized object and bringing it into the realm of ideas. The encounter with the audience was always key, the experience of the work of art a premium concern.

Some of the earliest historical markers of installation art date back to Marcel Duchamp's "readymades" and to the Surrealist exhibitions of the 1930s. Bringing mundane objects from the outside world into the gallery drew to attention the intangible values of the gallery space, the naming of something as art, and the power of the artist to imbue something with intent, giving it a significance that it did not otherwise have in the world outside of the gallery. In effect, the naming of a non-art object as "art" was the equivalent of placing that object on a plinth, repositioning it, and anointing it with some special abstract power. This very potent and tenacious principle has been used in commerce but in reverse, which is not with any subversive power, but for seduction. Branding is the supreme instance of this, as it brings to the commodity a kind of guarantee of worth. In both cases, however, the values entrusted to the object—of fashion or of art—are extrinsic as opposed to intrinsic to it. As with installation, the emphasis lies on the place and the encounter, and there is a tacit agreement between the installation and the viewer.

Despite a series of earlier instances of installation, the main historical watershed comes in the 1960s with Minimalism. Minimalism when applied to fashion generally refers to garments that are sparing with ornament, subdued and limited in color, and with a discernibly linear and simplified silhouette. These are reductivist tenets that are applied to all forms of utilitarian design. Minimalism in art, while also pared down and geometric, is an approach that occurred in the wake of the boom of Abstract Expressionism in the 1950s. The most influential essay, to the point of impassability as no lengthy discussion can be had without it, is Michael Fried's "Art and Objecthood" (1967) in which he now famously criticized Minimalism for its "theatricality."[4] Good art, Fried held, was "absorptive," it transported the viewer rather than drawing attention to itself. He cites the sculptor Tony Smith who, when asked about the size of his works, replies, "I was not making a monument . . . I was not making an object."[5] Instead, the work was designed to act in concert with the body. Its temporality was as something irrepressibly present of the moment, hence theatrical. Minimal art not only drew attention to the act of beholding but also to the surrounding architecture. In the words of Julian Rose, "A human-sized sculpture, neither too small nor too large, invites the viewer to move around it, gaining a full understanding through exploration of a shared space."[6] Moreover, the mute opacity of the Minimalist object amplifies this experience, such that even the modulations of light, or the scuff-marks and similar chance interruptions on the surface on the object count as part of the experience. Minimalism is the advent of the installation as a practice of art as well as a way of thinking about art, because with Minimalism everything becomes sculpture, everything is an object. This means that installation is not only a practice (as per someone who refers to him- or herself as an "installation artist"), but it implies a linguistic and epistemic shift in the art object. The painting is no longer the illusion of two dimensions, but a three-dimensional block, however slender, on the wall. Exhibitions were no longer "put up" or "bumped in" but installed, whereby the arrangement and distribution of art objects were taken into account as driving a significant part of the way in which they were understood. Seen in this way, installation implies an activation of space, whose effects can be docilely decorative to outright political. Activation can be ambient, or it can come as a result of what is barely visible. Michael Heizer's *Double Negative* (1970) involved displacing almost a quarter of a million tons of sandstone forming an oblong trench in the canyon of Moapa Valley in Nevada. The art "object" is defined precisely by the absent substance; it is the void described by the very substantial rocky formations. Intent and scale are very significant here, for to attempt the same on a piece of Plasticine is hardly consequential, while to go to such great lengths to perform, from a logical point of view, such a gratuitous act is highly provocative. The void thus described pulsates with something ineffable. The space is strikingly activated.[7]

By now, it is evident that installation draws on just as much that is intangible and ineffable as it does on the tangible and articulable. There is frequently a strong emphasis placed on the passing of time and the mobility of space. While one chief motivation for this was, from the 1960s onward, economic in as much as the artwork was difficult or impossible to sell, another was to perturb and destabilize the certainty in perceptual and affective categories (a perturbation that in fashion installation would noticeably take place in destabilizing presumed gender categories). A favored approach was to set up relationships that revealed dead-ends and inequities. Mary Kelly's *Post-Partum Document* (1973–1979) is a large series of works whose subject is her relationship to her son. Kelly uses a multitude of approaches in which various acts, responses, feelings, and experiences are mapped and subjected to rigorous and systematic scrutiny. In so doing, Kelly subjects one of the most, if not the most, physical and emotional experiences to a series of modalities that attempt to reduce it to material and comprehensive units. One of the outcomes was to expose the limits, and/or merits, of the rigors imposed on the mother–child relationship. Although the work was installed traditionally, as framed pinned objects on a gallery wall, it was these conventions that were also put into play, as the artist herself explains:

> I felt it was crucial to consider now the work intervened in a particular institutionalized context. So, in a sense, the way it looks in the gallery is an important consideration. On the one hand, it appears to be a record of external events, but on the other, it doesn't function in that space as simply a document; the installation is intended to construct several readings or ways through the text.[8]

While it is a commonplace that a thorough understanding of art entails sensitivity to the different ways it is historically construed or seen according to the individual viewer, what is at stake in Kelly's words is the manner in which the work actively *solicits* multiple readings. The Archimedian point, where there might be some ideal and as-yet-unreachable "faithful" and authentic reading of the work is jettisoned in favor of the opposite. Installation at its best is imbued with some kind of absence, an absence whose equivalent lies in the decentered subject.[9] Not only does no object exist, but claims as to the autonomy of genres could only be upheld historically (as in painting as an historical accumulation of historical examples), but no longer phenomenally.

Unmooring art from the age-old genres to the single sphere of the object caused many artists no longer to discriminate between disciplines, and to range freely across them. And practices once considered so different, such as performance and sculpture, were seen as having similar properties and having the ability to convey similar ideas. In the 1960s, Robert Morris engaged with performance art as well as fabricated objects, while Robert Rauschenberg (not a Minimalist) created "combines," turning a bed into painting (1955), or used his own body as moving, spiraling sculpture (*Elgin Tie*, 1964). As Rosalind Krauss explains, it was during this period that artists from both Europe and America

> became interested both in theater and in the extended experience of time which seemed part of the conventions of the stage. From this interest came some sculpture to be used as *props* in productions of dance and theater, some to function as *surrogate performers*, and some to act as the on-stage generators of scenic effects.[10]

There was a sizeable redefinition of the object whereby the static and fabricated object became imbricated with the body, which in certain instances by certain performers could also become an object. One notable case is Marina Abramovic and Ulay's *Imponderabilia* (1977), where they stood naked facing one another flanking the entrance of a museum. The experimental choreographer Yvonne Rainer stipulated that dance be catalyzed by "some *thing*" as opposed to "oneself," thereby removing the particular subjectivity of the processes of orchestrated movement.[11] The cross-relation between the systematic, doll-like body and the body-doll of the *mannequin* could not be more evident. And yet, as Rainer later claims, "My *Trio A* dealt with the 'Seeing' difficulty by dint of its continual and unremitting revelation of gestural detail that did not repeat itself, thereby focusing on the fact that the material could not easily be encompassed."[12] That the "material could not easily be encompassed" could be used as something of a coda for this book, since at the heart of installation and performance are the multiple perspectives of space and the unrepeatability in time of the event. Even in reproduction, the language of installation is the lived component, the point of view and an always-shifting—un-encompassable—set of components and perspectives. Installation reasserts the embodied and temporal qualities essential to experiencing, and the experience of, fashion.[13]

Fashion and installation

In the 1960s, the worlds of fashion and art were significantly apart, with some notable exceptions such as Andy Warhol and his conglomerate of misfits and models who congregated around his studio, "The Factory," which occupied various venues around mid-town Manhattan. But it is precisely art's continued "objecthood" that drew art and fashion closer together. Once Minimalism ceased to have the same critical, subversive edge it had in the 1960s, by the 1980s it was a diluted style that was taken up by collectors, where terms such as "slick" were not necessarily pejorative, alas. Writing in 2001, T. J. Clark claims that "the forms of representation" or modernism "are now unreadable. Or readable only under some dismissive fantasy rubric—of 'purism', 'opticality', 'formalism', 'elitism', etc.)"[14] One reason for this stylistic perturbation and exhaustion has been, admittedly, the way that fashion popularizes anything worth popularizing, with no scruples about turning anything into a fad and a catchphrase. But while art has become more and more like fashion, there are tendencies within the fashion industry that have harnessed artistic practices to their own ends, whose profitability is not only monetary but critical. As we have argued in a recent book, there are designers that can be cited as having a practice that is as critically incisive, if not more so, than artists.[15] One way they have done this is to rethink traditional modes of displaying and presenting fashion, either eliminating the body, to subsuming the garment under the extravagant pageantry of the event (the "catwalk").

Many such examples are to be explored in this book, but let us take but one example by way of clarifying the definition of fashion installation, Alexander McQueen's Fall/Winter collection for 2001, "What a Merry-Go-Round," a catwalk unjustly overshadowed by the "Voss," which directly precedes it. Staged on an actual merry-go-round site, the atmosphere is chillingly dark and mysterious. The make-up artist, Val Garland, who also worked on various other McQueen collections, painted the models as sad clowns, transforming them into something uninvitingly ghastly and vampiric. This was McQueen's *Danse Macabre* of fashion, suggesting a world where childhood innocence is replaced with melancholy and mourning. The music was the "Child Catcher" song from *Chitty Chitty Bang Bang*, not from the original but newly composed the same year as the collection launch.[16] The models slink languidly like dissociated, uncanny automata around the merry-go-round, as the henchwomen or surrogates for the Child Catcher himself. To avoid any ambiguity, one model drags behind her a shining brass skeleton. As we will also see in the case of "Voss," "What a Merry-Go-Round" was also a critical meditation on the fashion industry. Writing on what she calls the "fashion circus," Caroline Evans comments that "although the circus is a locus of spectacle, fun and abandon, it is also a twilight world of refuge, danger and loss of self,"[17] something that McQueen's event amplifies to a stirring, and almost perplexing, degree. The collection itself had a dark clown-like edge, interspersed with overt references to death, such as the black knit with a death's head. Other garments had angular harlequin-like patterns, and a dress used tutu tulle. It was clear that these garments were telling some kind of story, functioning like pieces in a larger psychological puzzle. It was a world of fallen and jaded entertainers, whores, pimps, and gangsters. There were suits with a distinctly Zoot-like inspiration, and enlarged, baggy vests were worn almost like armless coats. The models used a pole on which to turn, pole-dancer style, but something lent an air of grotesquerie to those in semi-drag. In many respects, this catwalk provided a profound insight into high fashion and the industries that present and represent it: we the audience marvel at the elegance and confident mastery of the spectacle, admiring a degree of panache and fantasy of which our everyday lives of expedients are a bad copy. Meanwhile, the figures that give us this delight and incite our envy and desire are merely ciphers, clowns, puppets in an act, condemned to an eternal return of acting out someone else's play, and for the sake of others. "What a Merry-Go-Round" was a critical comment that the "space of fashion" is therefore that zone that exists between these two states of imagined reality.

An important caveat needs to be made at this juncture. The more common term for events like McQueen's, with their distinctively operatic staging, is "performance," and although adequate to some degree (as in historically unspecific uses of words like "romantic" and "avant-garde"), it is an incomplete definition that privileges the temporal and bodily components. Whereas, as we saw in, say, Kelly's use of the term, "installation" is an elastic term for the ways in which art, and now fashion, objects are provided conceptual settings by which to expose and provoke meanings that are open-ended, critical, and inimical to accepted opinion. Take, for example, the work of American fashion designer Rick Owens, whose creative practice moves across disciplines from fashion to object and furniture design as well as sculpture. Although we have examined Owen's in detail,[18] it is worth mentioning here that he is one of the few designers whose modes of installation cross open-ended, closed, and *still* displays. For his 2014 Spring/Summer collection show "Vicious," Owens used largely mixed-race, plus-sized models who stomped around the catwalk scowling at the audience and beating their chests to a club techno and tribal drum beat. The open-ended performance culminated in what seemed like a war dance by an Amazonian cult. Similarly, Owens used an open-ended installation for his ready-to-wear Spring/Summer 2016 that he aptly titled "Cyclopes." Models were sent down the catwalk carrying other models strapped upside down on their bodies as if they were rucksacks. The concept was a simple one, a nod to sisterhood in the fight for women's liberation, as women, literally, carried each other on their backs. Subversive acts and large-scale nudity are common features of Owens' *still* installations that comprise sculptures, furniture, and garments. In 2006, Owens commissioned the artisan Doug

Jennings from Madame Tussauds wax museum in London to produce a series of life-sized sculptures which he included in his *Dustdam and Dustpump* installation at the Uomo Pitti Imaginaire fashion fair in Florence. The wax sculpture was a life-size replica of Owens with his jeans unzipped, holding his penis whilst urinating onto a rug of sand and mirrors. Bodily excretions feature quite heavily in Owens' work, most recently for his first retrospective, "Subhuman, Inhuman, Superhuman" (2018), held at the Triennale di Milano, where a giant turd sculpture, made up in part from Owens' hair, hung suspended in the entrance to the gallery space. The sculpture is in reference to a comment that Owens made nearly thirty years ago, that he would "lay a black glittering turd on the white landscape of conformity."[19]

Art installation can be with bodies and without them; as we will see, this is the same for fashion. There is also an important semantic distinction between fashion installation catwalks and theatrical and operatic staging, namely that with the latter the clothing is as costume subordinated to the philosophical and narrative trajectory of the piece. The costumes are integers of the interpretation of a particular script, or improvisatory setting. By stark contrast, fashion installation is defined by varying degrees of tension in its relation to the body and the garment. It is a tension that is self-evident when the body is absent, but also when models do not follow accepted, habitual norms of body type, body shape, or gender. With respect to installation and the catwalk, often the aesthetic forcefulness of the event—the set or the site, the choreography, the music, or a combination of all of these—will overshadow the clothes, and intentionally so. It is a rendering absent, or obscure, that in turn instigates rather than mutes desire. It engenders mystique, intrigue, allure. And from the very outset, the designer signals levels of the garment's disappearance, and that its readings are seamless and consistent with a set of factors that are both in and out of his or her control. It is this placing that is the *installation* of fashion into a uneven web of contexts, expectations, and constructs, and which ensures that fashion is preserved as something flexible and fluid that presides over the changeability of time, place, and identity.

The architecture of this book

This book follows a largely dialectical, tripartite structure comprising of roughly three parts: "Body", "Space", and "Body-in-Space". Chapter 1, "Body: *mise en scène*," looks at the beginning of fashion through the lens of its staging, including the sites and spaces through which fashion was viewed and consumed. Indeed, installation is a useful way in which to begin to understand the fashion system as it emerged in the mid-nineteenth century. With

Frederick Worth, Jean Patou, Elsa Schiaparelli, Coco Chanel, and Paul Vionnet, the catwalk becomes an important way in which fashion is consumed, and as such, there began to be increasing reflection on the nature of the site and the staging. What were once the invisible supports for consumption were brought into closer relief. It is also in the early twentieth century with Poiret that we see the invention of the first fashion shoot (photographed by Steichen), and hence the growing emphasis on scene, narrative, and atmosphere. An important point of reference for this examination of the early stages is the work of Walter Benjamin and his *Passagen-Werk*, and his celebrated analysis of the vitrines in the arcades as encapsulating discrete "dream worlds." The reference to Benjamin is important as it is intrinsic to understanding the relation between later fashion installation and the constructed, synthetic worlds (well before the term was ever coined in relation to works of art) that he observed in the Paris arcades. This leads to a broader discussion of the environments created for selling fashion and luxury goods in the early department stores, such as Harrods, Selfridges, and Bloomingdale's. It is also noteworthy that the presentation of fashion in shop windows long predates the fashion curator's predicament of exhibiting fashion without the living body.

The next chapter, "Fashion (almost) without bodies," begins with a description of McLaren and Westwood's various stores, and then Westwood alone, in terms of what has already been discussed above. This will also provide the platform for studies of fashion boutiques, such as the Rei Kawakubo's Dover Street Market in London and New York, Ralph Lauren's concept stores on Madison Avenue, New York, and the Hermès pop-up stores in Hong Kong and New York. The Burberry flagship store in Shanghai provides customers with runway shows and entertainment on interactive mirrors and digital screens. In each case, the designers convey through the display of fashion a distinct aesthetic experience. The chapter will also analyze various catwalks in the last fifteen to twenty years in terms of their set design, that is, in the absence of bodies and as baroque environments.

A series of catwalks in recent years by Christian Dior bears this concept out, even to the extent that the settings in their operatic grandeur threaten to eclipse the collections themselves. For the Fall/Winter collection 2015/2016, the audience sat within an immense structure consisting of layered and perpendicular decorative frames supported by metal frames and beams. The panels were largely of translucent green flecked with crimson, giving the feeling of sitting within a vast garden with the proportions of a jungle. For the Summer 2016 collection by Dior, the audience sat in a pristine white room gazing at a hillock littered with green foliage and lavender-colored flowers rising from one side of the room. At the base and center of the "landscape" was a white door from which the models spilled out. The minimal white starkness of the rest of the room, contrasting with the color and resplendence of the spectacle, prompted the inevitable conclusion that the collection emanated from an otherworldly paradise. These are but two examples of others that will be detailed in this chapter of discrete installation environments that, while serving as a stage for the presentation of the collections, have their own aesthetic autonomy.

The final chapter brings the two themes together, especially as witnessed in the last twenty or so years, when fashion is displayed and consumed as part of an elaborate multiform pageant, or *Gesamtkunstwerk*. Generally translated as "total work of art," the term was used by Richard Wagner for his own operatic creations, which he believed were the apogee of artistic conception, bringing all the arts—poetry, drama, painting, sculpture, and music—into one transcendent whole. The term was later revived in the 1990s with new media theory, to characterize works such as single- or multi-channel video installations. It is not only an apt term for catwalks such as McQueen's described above, but also for the advent of fashion film in the twenty-first century.

Divided into two parts, this chapter will look at the all-encompassing catwalk shows in terms of their formal structure: open and closed. The open form is where the audience is almost part of the catwalk, making the boundaries porous, such as for McQueen's Spring/Summer 1997 catwalk show "Untitled" (also known as "Golden Shower," the sexual act of partners urinating over each other) where the audience, models, and photographers were drenched in a downpour of liquid. This open form of fashion installation brings together theatrical performance, fashion, and art. John Galliano's models often encourage audience participation in his runway shows, for Fall/Winter 1997 musicians and performers entertained the crowd and were part of the catwalk production. Again, Jean Paul Gaultier's Fall/Winter 1992 collection, "La Poupée," took place in a railway carriage where the audience acted as passengers.

The other type of catwalk show is closed: where the audience feels that it is gazing at a different world. The first is more theatrical such as Gareth Pugh's immersive installation film directed by Ruth Hogben and screened at Uomo Pitti Imaginaire (2011) as part of his collection, which was based on religious iconography. The film was screened on the domed ceiling of an eleventh-century basilica, immersing the audience into a mythological world of demi-gods. The closed show also maintains cinematic effects, drawing the viewer into a different world with the use of senses such as touch and smell, transporting them into an imaginary and seductive place. Ralph Lauren's immersive four-dimensional experience is a prime example of the convergence of film, cinematic technologies such as green screens, and fashion. To celebrate the brand's historical trajectory, Ralph Lauren used cinematic effects and digital technology to project a film on the New York women's flagship store on Madison Avenue. Using screen effects, the film created the illusion of a folding building that opened and closed, transforming into a series of objects, including perfume bottles that sprayed scent onto the participating audience. For the launch of his Summer/Spring 2015 Polo womenswear collection, Ralph Lauren created a show that celebrated New York by projecting the film onto a sixty-foot-tall water fountain in Central Park. Similarly for the launch of their flagship store in Shanghai, Burberry shipped an entire steam train to the city and projected an interactive film on the exterior of the building that highlighted Burberry's heritage and innovation.

The closed cinematic spaces also belong to the scenes used in fashion films where the body acts as an interloper between worlds. Moving images, or fashion films, provide designers and fashion brands with an immersive aesthetic, which summarizes their identity or the collection's concept. This narrative style is favored by brands such as Kenzo, Chanel, and Gucci that explore the sartorial heritage of their brand through the medium; others, such as Eckhaus Latta, use found video clips and nature documentaries sliced together in an experimental way. To this we also add the notion of *still* fashion installations, which are those that operate the entire sensory field of the viewer, an immersive, consuming experience that expels any consideration of the outside world.

The ambition of this book is to advance a concept by defining it. From a contemporary perspective, words such as "performance" and "conceptual" only do part of the job to describe the complex ways fashion is presented and represented today. Just as the body–clothing division is a specious one, fashion no longer, if ever, exists in isolation, and is not reducible to the garment. Rather, fashion finds itself installed within codes, images, ideologies, narratives; some of them invented, others latent. We are very much returned to the oft-cited etymology of "text," from the Latin *textus*, meaning "woven" (from the verb *textere*). The fashion garment is inseparably woven into the fabric of images and ideas, in a manner that is as mobile and alive as the body that wears it.

1

BODY
MISE EN SCÈNE

In 1937, *Stage* magazine ran an advertisement for the perfume *Chanel No. 5*:

> Madame Gabrielle Chanel is above all an artist in living. Her dresses, her perfumes are
> created with a faultless instinct for drama. Her perfume #5 is like the soft music that
> underlies the playing of a love scene. It kindles the imagination; indelibly fixes the scene
> in the memories of the players.[1]

The saccharine mawkishness of the passage should not be a complete deterrent, as there are several relevant themes latent within it, albeit not devised with any philosophical intention. It begins with describing Chanel's art as living, implying lifestyle but also all the things that bring quality to the lived moment. Her creations add and assert a quality to life that makes life more acute. Their "drama" insists upon play and performance; they set the wearer on a stage of style and desire. Chanel's famous perfume thrusts its users into a narrative that is then burned upon their respective memories. The last word, "players," leaves no doubt about the way in which Chanel brings her consumers into a realm of enactment. Chanel was the first couturier not only to create a signature fragrance, but also to use it to fill her fitting rooms at the rue Cambon with its ambience, a practice revived by recent designers such as Thierry Mugler, whose boutiques are aggressively "Angelified" as a branding exercise to promote his perfume, *Angel*.

With such gestures and ruses, Chanel was one of a number of designers who effectively helped to inaugurate the scenic model of fashion that has gained in density and sophistication ever since. Perfume's very intangibility and ineffability, yet the power of the olfactory organ to evoke and connote, brings us directly to the very core of fashion as encircled by images, and the extent to which glamour and prestige are abstract and immaterial. Contemporary advertising of perfume drives this notion home, for any effort to describe the perfume, which would be absurd, is replaced by an arbitrary association with a place or a celebrity that is made to seem indelible. Whether it is the mystique of a place or the magnetism of a known personality, the perfume is a confirmation of desirability and a fabricated world made abstractly concrete. Whereas clothing and accessories are concrete and have their uses, perfume's only palpable elements are its color (if any) and the shape of the bottle it is in. Yet it is precisely because perfume is untethered to the world of things that makes it the optimal example of the narrative worlds that circulate around commodities. For the rise of fashion display is indissolubly part of the rise of commodity culture and the spectacle, from the birth of the modern department store to the birth of film. The *mise en scène* of fashion is to be viewed together with the beginning of large-scale public exhibitions, such as the Great Exhibition in London in 1851, and the Exposition Universelle in Paris in 1855. National display is historically symmetrical with personal display. Personal mobility and reinvention is to be understood only according to the inventions of fashion itself, whereby the garment's semantic strength was owed to innumerable other properties brought to it through its presentation and display.

Exhibitions, arcades, and department stores

In the days of artisans and guilds, there was a more "authentic" relationship to manufacture and selling, with the artisan selling the things they made in the shop designated for that purpose. In pre-modern times, those who only sold and did not make were peddlers, who were deemed inferior to those who made things. But by the nineteenth century, salespeople, the middlemen between producer and consumer, were often those who benefited more than those at the center of production. It became the skill of salespeople not only to act convincingly, but also to provide environments that cast prospective consumers into places commensurate to dreams. This was the insight of Walter Benjamin, who in his vast and unfinished work, *The Arcades Project* [*Das Passagen-werk*], perceived the close connection between museums, places of leisure (clubs, spas), and arcades. In the arcades, shopping need not be entirely a material experience but was a mental one as well (Figure 1). Benjamin refers to "Dream houses of the collective: arcades, winter gardens, panoramas, factories, wax museums, casinos, railway stations."[2] Moreover, "Arcades are houses or passages having no outside—like the dream."[3] In another entry, Benjamin writes of "the dreaming collective, which through the arcades, communes with its insides. We must follow in its wake so as to expound the nineteenth century—in fashion and advertising, in buildings and politics—as the outcome of its dream visions."[4] Benjamin saw an undeniable connection between what his friend Ernst Bloch would characterize as hopefulness for collective better life in the configurations of modern life. Modern life placed people and commodities in settings that literally staged the promise of greater possibility.

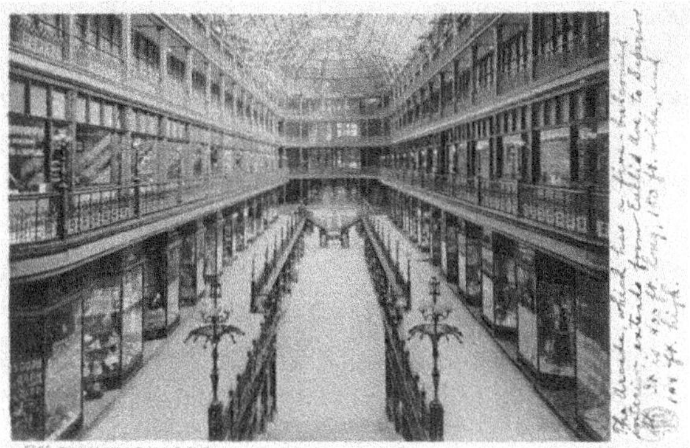

Figure 1 The Arcade, Cleveland, Ohio.

In his chapter on the dream in Benjamin's work, Eli Friedlander insightfully writes that:

An environment is essentially different from an object given to consciousness, it cannot be simply identified, broken into parts, isolated, and studied. The manifestation of the incorporation of an environment in consciousness would make certain images stand for or gather the amorphous surroundings. These are the dream images. . . . The deformation of the dream images is the manifestation of the internalization in the arcades. The arcades provide a gathering point in wish images of the yet-to-be articulated environment of life.[5]

For Benjamin, these dream-images were meant to transform into a new configuration of consciousness that could lead to an "awakening" to fulfill the utopian goals of humanity.[6]

Fashion, however, could also be distrusted because it manipulated such dreams and desires for its own ends. The utopianism was built into its rhetoric but not as an earnest philosophical program. And the conflation of commodities with dreams has relevance to this day, but was most evident when it came to fashion. "Fashion," Benjamin remarks, "like architecture, inheres in the darkness of the lived moment, belongs to the dream consciousness of the collective. The latter awakes, for example, in advertising."[7] Benjamin, although revealing at times an ambivalence to fashion, was also encouraged by his friendship with Helen Hessel, with whom he visited fashion shows and whose book *Vom Wesen der Mode* [On the Nature of Fashion] he read with great interest and cited in his notes on the arcades.[8]

Benjamin's musings on the panorama will also prove relevant to later, more contemporary examples of fashion installation. What makes Benjamin's work significant is that it is the most developed and intricate set of reflections on the spectacle of modernity and the agonistic relationship between the perennial and ephemera. "The historical object," note Howard Eiland and Michael Jennings, "citing past and future simultaneously, like any object of fashion, unfolds as palimpsest and picture puzzle."[9] Fashion exists together with and against other fashions, as well as the linguistic–historical conditions of placement, use, and association.

As a tendentious manipulation of ethnicity and history, the Great Exhibition of 1851 had a lasting effect on all manner of the ways things were displayed. Ethnicity was put on show, but just as preponderantly, fashion. On display were not only countless forms of ethnic dress, items of fashion, but also the public themselves (Figure 2). As Alistair O'Neill explains, the educative, even didactic, environment of the Great Exhibition proved appealing:

The premise of learning about fashion through its educational display was a new proposition that women's interest titles sought to unpack, offering commentaries on articles of dress, textiles for dress and accessories displayed in the Great Exhibition distinct from those found in official and popular published guides. Another special quality is their captured sense of visiting the exhibition, as journey and route, attraction and edification, as an experience tailored.[10]

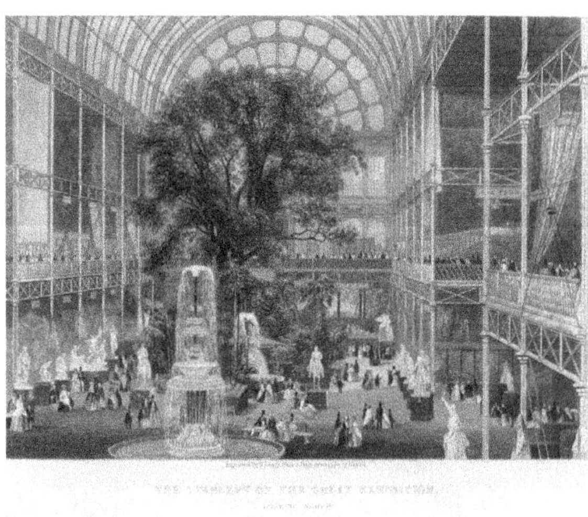

Figure 2 The transept of the Great Exhibition (looking north), held in London in 1851.

What the Great Exhibition helped to nurture and to isolate was the essential yet most elusive of constituents, namely that fashion is an experience that unfolds when bodies, clothing, and environments meet. It presented many items of clothing not for sale, but clearly with the intent of ensuring that they would be in the ostensibly different, but in fact deeply related, context of the store (Figure 3). Helped as well by the accompanying guides and the reports made on such displays in women's magazines, the displays, while under the sobering guise of guidance and instruction, were sites of temptation, where visitors could gather for themselves their own internal wish images which they would then realize for themselves outside the exhibition. To extrapolate Benjamin's insight, the more self-evident dream-world of the exhibition helped to mask the dream-world of the shopping arcade and the department store.

By the opening years of the twentieth century, the expectations around the level of fanfare in the European Great Exhibitions reached new heights, as had the zeal with which such expectations were met. For the 1900 Exposition Universelle in Paris, fashion was one of the central features, that is, fashion and its surrounding mood and narrative settings. This was the exhibition that sought to launch France as the leader of the pan-European, if not international, style of Art Nouveau, and was therefore rich in design and the inherent stagecraft of the style that melded eighteenth-century nostalgia with the still relatively new frenzy for Japonism. The estimated fifty million people who visited the Chambre Syndicale would have seen a fashion hall divided into four units, each symbolizing

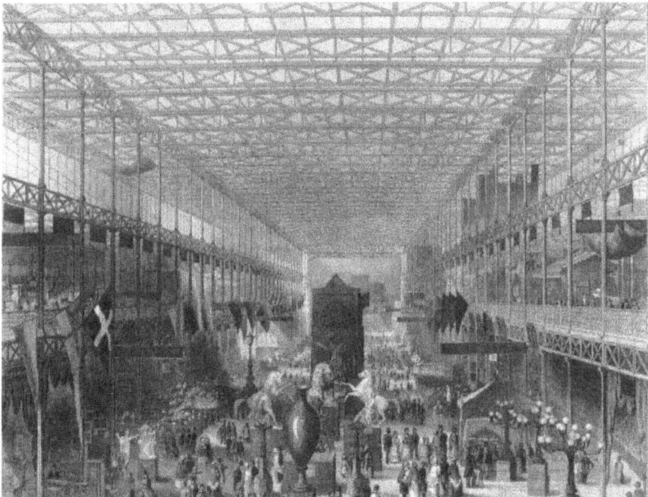

Figure 3 The nave of the Great Exhibition (looking west), held in London in 1851.

the four seasons. In the words of Amy De La Haye: "Autumn was represented by the Longchamps races; the great hall of a luxurious private house evoked Winter; Spring featured a *defile* (fashion show); and Summer depicted the seaside resort of Deauville."[11] The couturiers drew lots for where they would exhibit. Jean Worth, who had drawn Fall and Summer, was tentative as to how sympathetic the themes would be to his more stately designs. His brother Gaston followed the allocated themes, while Jean thought better and set about his own schema, which was a sensation of sumptuousness. In Jean Worth's own words:

> In this I put a copy of a Louis XVI drawing-room and staged therein incidents from English life. The models represented a great lady dressed in the regulation court costume, three feathers and all, with her young sister whom she was to represent to the queen; a lady reclining on the sofa in a splendid tea gown, her tiny sister offering tea to her guests: a maid holding a *manteaux de soirée*; a lady in a white *tailleur* . . . These fragments of scenes allowed the use of all materials from cloth to brocade, and all styles from the most elaborate to the uniform of the maid. Yet they were fitted out with due regard to reality that those who saw the set could not exclaim enough over it. Its sensation was such that it became necessary to station a policeman before it in order to keep the crowd moving and during the six months the Exposition endured it was necessary to replace the floor twice.[12]

Crucial here is the claim of the "due regard to reality" that led to "exclamations" of delight. In this regard, the connection between display and commodity has changed little. This is suggestion of verisimilitude in a wish image: the once closed, private, rarified world of the nobility and royalty is offered for all to see, for all to consume visually, and for all to delude themselves that they too could inhabit such a world. "You can be there, you can have that." And it is the schism between not having and the (ever delayed) possibility of having where dreams are made.

The connections between the Great Exhibitions and the department store were so close as to appear collusive. For like the exhibitions themselves, which offered ample opportunities to contemplate the wonders and magnificence of the world, department stores, as Joanne Entwistle observes, "were also places in which to sit around and dream."[13] One of the best examples of this was Aristide Boucicaut's Bon Marché in Paris, established in 1852, a year after the Great Exhibition in London, and just three years before its equivalent in Paris, in 1855. "Not only were prices clearly displayed as they had been at the Paris exhibition, but the shop's whole environment was created to be a spectacle, encouraging leisurely browsing." It was this experiential nature of fashion and consumption, and the inner experience of "browsing," that led Benjamin to draw the connection with the flâneur, Baudelaire's wanderer through the streets of Paris. The flâneur's consumption was not material but in sights, sounds, and smells, which were then poetically recomposed in his imagination. He is not just a figure or type, but an embodiment of the consciousness of the modern spectator, and the idea that the corresponding, complementary dimension of the commodity is the spectacle (something that Guy Debord would develop in his highly influential work from 1967, *The Society of the Spectacle*). Thus, as Benjamin comments, "The flâneur is the observer of the marketplace. His knowledge is akin to the occult science of industrial fluctuations. He is a spy of the capitalists, on assignment in the realm of consumers."[14] The consciousness and evolution of the flâneur also reveals that fashion exists across multiple surfaces of spectatorship, where wearer and observer are intertwined.[15]

Just as enmeshed in the display, consumption, and conception of fashion were advances in technology, specifically lighting. Lighting opened up whole new possibilities, for example, for more open spaces, and also for generating effects that created fairy-tale worlds that would stimulate desire. While the eighteenth century saw the entry of the enticing shop front to lure in a growing number of consumers as a result of a swelling middle class, advances in lighting at the end of the nineteenth century allowed for the illumination of large spaces. As Entwistle affirms, "Shop display became increasingly important in the late nineteenth century."[16] Ironically enough, one of the most voluble advocates of shop display in the United States was the near universally known author of *The Wonderful Wizard of Oz*, Frank Baum. "Baum's philosophy," Entwistle continues, "evident in his fairy-tales and his interest in merchandizing, celebrated consumption, display and artificial spectacle."[17] He even founded the first magazine entirely about window display, entitled *Shop Window*, where his interest in dream worlds, expressed in his children's books, found yet another expressive outlet. As Entwistle states: "He saw the importance of display in attracting the attention of passers-by and in stimulating desire for consumption." He played a significant role in transforming shop windows from simple, analogue as it were, display zones to apertures to imaginary worlds (Figure 4). Christopher Breward argues that the large amount of scholarship about sites of fashion consumption that rose from the middle of the nineteenth century has "tended to emphasize their fantastic and other-worldly character," thereby setting "off balance any attempt to define the material nature of consumer demand."[18] In this regard, fashion, as with every other commodity, was inserted into a narrative realm, something that to this day would have an irrepressible hold on the way fashion is consumed and understood. Fast forward to an example from the consumption of menswear in the 1980s, Entwistle states that "an important part of the selling of new styles for men was their location in particular sites of consumption that were consciously designed." In other words, a central feature of fashion's consumption was as a result of fashion installation.

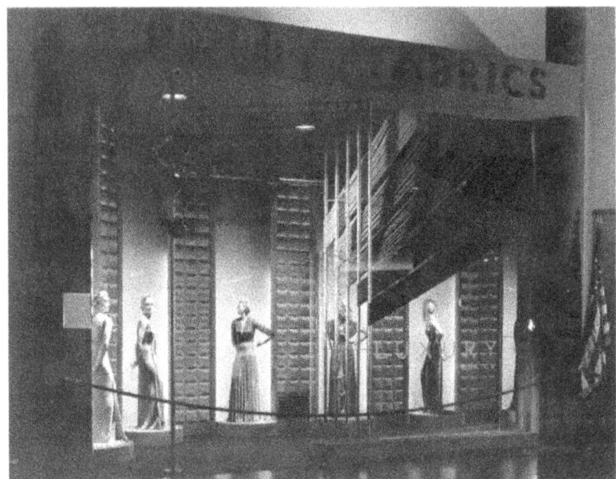

Figure 4 The world of mannequins: in velvet gowns in window displays.

Fashion display versus art display

Discussions of the rise of the way fashion display concurred with its consumption, while correlating strongly with the Great Exhibitions in Europe and later in the United States,[19] have tended not to make the connection with the way art was displayed in the same period. This is a strange oversight, not least because the parallels are striking, but also because the art of the second half of the nineteenth century and into the twentieth reflected the specular nature of society in numerous ways, in both its content and in the nature of exhibitions. While we do need to consider the origins of museums and "permanent" collections as such, the predominant emphasis is on transient exhibitions, ones that we can retrospectively say were installed and de-installed. It is also the temporariness of these exhibitions that aligns them to the transience associated more commonly to fashion.

The origins of the artistic display date back to the founding of the Paris Salon which began as "Academy of Painting and Sculpture" [*Académie de Peinture et Sculpture*] by Louis XIV's chief minister, Cardinal Mazarin, in 1648, with the first exhibition held in 1673. The celebration of culture had a highly pragmatic, almost cynical edge. For these exhibitions served the useful purpose of bringing artists together to compete against one another for medals, which meant in turn that the kings and other wealthy nobility no longer had to seek out the best talent, since it automatically came to them. (A similar arrangement was intended with Versailles, a place where the king could keep his eye on the nobility, who were too preoccupied plotting against one another instead of against him.) The equivalent in fashion is the Chambre Syndicale de la Haute Couture, which was founded in 1973 by Lucien Lelong. Chanel famously broke with the Chambre because of its strict gate-keeping policies to the kinds of people admitted to the fashion shows.[20] From 1725 onward, the Salon was held in the Louvre, and in 1737 it was opened to the public. (The British equivalent, the Royal Academy was established a little later in 1768. Between 1771 and 1836, Academy exhibitions were held in Somerset House, but access was restricted by an entry fee to vet out the less desirable (and more odorous) poor.)

The first collection open to the public was the Luxembourg Gallery, which opened its doors in 1750, but then only on Wednesdays and Saturdays, and only for three hours. The public museum as we know it today originated as a result of the French Revolution, which opened the Louvre in the summer of 1793, stating that the people were "rightful" owners of the treasures there.[21] Shortly after, non-permanent exhibitions came not only when Napoleon showed off his plunder from his military exploits, but also on the occasions when the Louvre's Salon Carré "had to be vacated," as Francis Haskell points out,

> for several weeks each year to enable living artists to continue their long-established practice of using it to show their new look to the public—that gave changing consignments of freshly arrived booty an indelible association with the temporary and, hence, with the notion of exhibition rather than the museum.[22]

This association was crucial as it mediated the work considerably, giving it the special and attractive power of novelty, an impermanence that amplified immediacy of the event. When it came to the artists' own temporary shows, the state auspicing of the museum, and indeed its history as a royal palace, added esteem to their work—an early example of the power or branding that the relevance of a site confers upon the art object. It is a relationship that is exploited freely by the world of fashion. A favored site in Paris for haute couture catwalk shows is the Grand Palais, the traditional venue for the blockbuster art exhibitions frequently partnered with other major museums such as the Metropolitan in New York.

The Grand Exhibitions of the middle of the nineteenth century stimulated many artists to offer alternative methods of marketing their work to a public that was being more and more groomed to respond to the spectacle. In 1855, coinciding with the Paris exhibition, Courbet stages his own personal retrospective. Such retrospectives forced a contextual and narratalogical reading, whereby viewers were made aware of the artist's evolution and maturation. The artist's body of work was literally offered to behold in a particular space, or spaces. According to Robert Jensen, however, this massing of an artist's work (with some carefully chosen comparisons with other great artists' works) had a de-historicizing effect: "Works of art are treated in retrospectives in relation to each other rather than externally to other art, to the cultural, social, and political issues that helped to form the artist's horizon of beliefs."[23] Indeed, "retrospectives operated on the principle of exclusion rather than inclusion, focusing attention only on the work of art as an isolated entity."[24] This displacement, or deracination, had, and has, a singularly narcissistic effect, something to which we will return in more recent practices which have also been seized upon in fashion installation.

Installation in art as it came to be understood since the 1970s began in earnest when artists themselves began to design exhibitions in the early twentieth century. An early forerunner of this was Monet in the 1890s, when he exhibited his series paintings (Rouen cathedral, the haystacks, poplars, mornings on the Seine) in such a way as to suggest that they are best apprehended as a corpus, or suite, than individually. This practice carried through to the *Water Lilies* cycle of paintings, which André Masson called the "Sistine Chapel of Impressionism" and which were installed in 1927 at the Orangerie in Paris, a year after the artist's death.[25] The avant-garde of the twentieth century took advantage of their outsider status to the sanctioned forums for art—even in cases where such exhibitions did have official, government support—by mounting exhibitions that had a self-conscious sense of their own theater, which tended to foreground the *lack* of neutrality of the intent of the work and the manner in which it was shown. A signal example of this was the Russian Constructivist El Lissitzky's design of the Soviet pavilion for the Pressa exhibition in Cologne in 1928. Having already begun designing pavilions for the Soviet Union in 1926, Lissitzky followed the example of the *Dada-Messe* in Berlin in 1920 where individual works were subordinated to an all-over environmental whole. Notably, as Jan Tschichold explains:

> With Lissitzky, all the possibilities of a new exhibition technique were explored: in place of a tedious succession of framework, containing dull statistics, he produced a new purely visual design of the exhibition space and its contents, by the use of glass, mirrors, celluloid, nickel, and other materials; by contrasting these newfangled materials with wood, lacquer, textiles and photographs; by the use of natural objects instead of pictures . . . by bringing a dynamic element into the exhibition by means of continuous films, illuminated and intermittent letters and a number of rotating models. *The room thus became a sort of stage on which the visitor himself seemed to be one of the players*. The novelty and vitality of the exhibition did not fail: this was proved by the fact that this section attracted by far the largest number of visitors, and had at times to be closed owing to overcrowding.[26]

Perhaps less palatable to the purist (not fashion) art-goer is that the exhibition was more consumed rather than contemplated, a spectacle of entertainment over the sober edification. But crucial too here is the manner in which the viewer-visitor was given the opportunity, or illusion, of having a participatory role in an environment that appeared to be deficient without an audience. Thus these kinds of exhibition arrangements were instrumental in breaking down the imaginary division between audience and display, and could be read as a measure in democratizing art. For most of the twentieth-century avant-garde, bringing art to the people was a primary concern. It is also easy to see why fashion would adopt installation for itself, given that fashion is also largely deficient without an active, live body. The participation and experiential dimensions are part of this.

Another citable example in the historical genealogy of installation was the design for the International Surrealist Exhibition in Paris that opened in January 1938 at George Wildenstein's Beaux-Arts Galleries in Paris (Wildenstein had also been Monet's dealer). Designed by André Breton and mostly by Marcel Duchamp, the works on exhibition were physically drowned out by traditional Surrealist devices such as mannequins, but less foreseen were 1,200 empty coal bags suspended from the ceiling of the central exhibition space. Beneath them, in the center of the room, was a coal brazier illuminated from within. In the words of Benjamin Buchloh, as a result of "vibrations caused by loudspeakers blasting German military marches, the sacks slowly and steadily released coal dust upon the visitors."[27] In his reading, the dust was a comment on the precipitous omens of fascism from Germany and Italy, while the brazier, used by Paris cafés during winter, "undoubtedly functioned as a similarly hilarious metonymy of the increasingly common Fascist mythification of *la flame*: flames, torches and fires."[28] Walking around in gloom only mitigated by the light of the brazier, visitors were given battery-powered flashlights to inspect the paintings. This ruse had the dual purpose of suggesting that the pungency of the Surrealist movement had all but died, as well as heightening the sense of prurience in inspecting the many images that availed themselves of sexual content.[29] Buchloh refers to Duchamp's installation as a "phantasmagoria of a fallen world."[30] Many such self-consciously artist-designed exhibitions prompt, according to Claire Grace, "a hybrid rethinking, from a class perspective, of concerns of materiality, agency, and the boundaries of art and mass culture."[31] Certainly, Duchamp's exhibition could claim to be challenging in its time, although his example, when a well-practiced approach by the end of the century, would more likely collude with the bugbear of art-as-entertainment.

Duchamp's audacious intervention would later be recalled in one of Joseph Beuys' last major works, *Plight* (1985), now permanently installed in the Museum of Modern Art (Centre Georges Pompidou) in Paris.[32] Viewers enter through a low door, being forced to stoop into a room that is lined with rolls of thick felt, which has a strong but muted smell, while changing the timbre of sounds to the effect of similarly changing the sense of one's own occupation of space. The infiltration of the mass of felt on the transmission of sound is rendered even more unsettling by the presence of a grand piano in the space, an inert symbol of power. Deriving after the calamity of World War II as opposed to before it, Beuys' work elicits a number of readings, high among them the disorienting and dehumanizing effect of concentration camps and the constant foreboding of death. By the time it was created, *Plight* was already an accepted form of artistic display, given that in the decade before, in the 1970s, "Happenings," performances, "Environments" were all strategies of audience engagement, as well as a form of aesthetic displacement that, among other things, sought to ensure that the art object was more of an experience in time and event which could not be appropriated as a commodity.

The other important development from experimental practices was video art, whose pertinence could not be greater today. Film is what Nick Knight refers to as the "Zeitgeist medium," which has superseded photography, a form that had its heyday in the 1980s and 1990s.[33] Growing availability of video data projectors has seen "video installation" become the norm, and the term "immersive environment" become accepted currency. In one of the earliest and among the most important meditations on video art and video installation, Rosalind Krauss reads video art as an elaborate form of narcissism, of the artist first then replicated onto the viewer.[34] In video installation, the viewer is regularly made aware of him- or herself through the shadow cast on the wall in the passage of walking in and around the space. She also acknowledges that video takes up "the temporal values that were built into Minimalist sculpture of the 1960s,"[35] where the viewer is made well aware of his or her presence and the process of decoding the work as it unfolds or moves in time. Narcissism is relevant on another level in as much as a video terminal brackets out the world, but even more so the video installation, where the room becomes an other-worldly sanctum.[36] Krauss is ambivalent about this, while fashion installation has exploited the narcissistic qualities and potential of multimedia environments to the nth degree. Body, garment, and environment appear on the catwalk as coming out of the gateway of a constructed world that weakens inhibition and stimulates desire.

The first modern catwalks and shows

The first fashion mannequins were by and large stationary, and their surroundings were deemed inconsequential to the garment itself. It was only soon after the establishment of the house of Worth that models began to take a more active role (the earliest surviving photograph of a live mannequin wearing a Worth gown dates from 1900). Before models were used in earnest and were allowed to show the garment in movement, until 1930 a popular alternative was a figure made of wax. These figures would have invariably been made in Paris by Pierre Imans of "Mannequins et Cires Artistiques" (Mannequins and Artistic Waxworks), who were renowned for the sharp, uncanny realism of their creations and their meticulous craftsmanship. For the 1911 International Exhibition in Turin, Imans exhibited and won a gold medal for a diorama of twelve well-attired men and women venturing to Lake Como. There are also photographic records of the House of Worth also using waxworks (presumably by Imans) in the early years of the twentieth century.[37]

Baudelaire's, and later Benjamin's, notion of the flâneur grew from a much more widely shared interest in being active, and of walking. In his *Arcades Project*, Benjamin has a large entry from Charles Blanc's "Considerations Regarding Womenswear," 1872 (*Considérations sur le vêtement des femmes*) in which he observes that the fashions of the Second Empire are more relaxed and inspire more vigorous outdoor activity: "Everything that could keep women from remaining seated was encouraged: anything that could have impeded their walking was avoided."[38] By the turn of the twentieth century, being active was seen as being part of the progress and bustle of modernity, and therefore being modern oneself. Despite the war, this futuristic ethos that joined mobility with velocity would continue to be invoked in the 1920s.[39] And for the fashion model to move, to go from A to B, was also then to prompt, ever so incipiently, a narrative. Narratives would eventuate into settings.

By 1900, designers would no longer confine mannequins to their houses, but send them into urban spaces. The Bois de Boulogne was a place of choice where mannequins ambled about in order to gauge the reactions of those around them. Unlike the nobility of the *ancien régime*, whose attitude to dress reflected their own autonomy and divine right, the modern body was consequent on others and on the places it inhabited; the body's presence and appearance was only as good as the sites it was in. In the same year, 1900, the fashion pavilion of the Exhibition featured wax mannequins in sumptuous surrounding tableaux. Although many deemed the wax dummies to be grotesque, the Exhibition was an important marker in the theatricalization of fashion.[40] In the last such Exhibition of 1937, the "Temple of Taste" included thirty fashion houses, including Lanvin, Chanel, Nina Ricci, Vionnet, and Patou. Michael Barker observes that "Dummies seems a rather crude word for the attenuated 'mannequins' stylishly modelled by the sculptor Robert Couturier (far removed from the ample female form of his master, Maillol) which were displayed in fantastical settings with an echo of de Chirico."[41] The elegant had mixed with the dreamily bizarre, perhaps as a final breath of escapism in anticipation of the years to follow.

In the 1900 Exhibition, the fashion exhibits were accompanied by cultural panoramas in which the world was miniaturized. As Benjamin comments: "On the world-travel panorama, which operated under the name 'Le Tour du Monde' at the Paris world exhibition of 1900, and which animated a changing panoramic background with living figures in the foreground, each time costumed accordingly."[42] With anthropology as with fashion, the human figure was clad so as to spark the imagination, and anticipate myriad hypothetical contexts and situations. Factuality and possibility, reality and dream, became indissoluble. The settings for bodies allowed for the external world to be turned inward, as Benjamin enigmatically states:

> The interest of the panorama in seeing the true city—the city indoors. What stands within the windowless house is the true, moreover, the arcade, too, is a windowless house. The windows that look down on it are like loges from which one gazes into its interior, but one cannot see out these windows to anything outside. (What is true has now windows; nowhere does the true look out to the universe.)[43]

Confounding inside and outside, the scenes of culture and of fashion were those of closed, monadic worlds that did not elicit doubt of conjecture.

The optimal medium for the reproduction of this dynamic was film, since film is both a convincing replication of the world as well as a closed world in itself. It was a double relationship that Benjamin intuited very well, and which he wrestled with in his artwork essay, especially on the conjecture of how film has the potential to free the masses as a means of communication, as much as to contain and enslave them, through propaganda.[44] Films of Paris fashion began circulating in 1910, and they were supportively received by a hungry American audience. In Weimar Germany of the 1920s, a new film genre surfaced, the *Konfektionskomödie*, or "fashion farce," one of the earlier precursors perhaps to today's fashion film, which occurred to support Germany's flourishing fashion industry. These typically took place in fashion houses, department stores, and during fashion parades. They attracted every level of society, from working women, to the well-to-do. The content generally followed familiar patterns, as Mila Ganeva relates, including

> the shrewd male shop assistant who knew how to cater to capricious and vain customers; and there was the ambitious, smart, indispensable female mannequin (*Konfektionsmädel*, *Probiermamsell*, *Gelbstern*, or *Konfektioneuse*), who hoped to acquire middle-class status, to become a "fashion queen" (*Modekönigin*), an actress, a film star, or an owner of a designer salon.[45]

The fusion of fashion and film provided an effective spectacle of modern life through the *Modenschau*, or fashion show, but built into discrete narrative form. For those who could not afford expensive fashions, they offered a surrogate experience.[46] As Ganeva concludes, the fashion show of early Weimar cinema "reflected (even in the most straightforward and trivial narratives) the experience of modernity, which is in essence the experience of an environment becoming increasingly distracting, disjunctive, and fragmented."[47] However, it was the encapsulation through the filmic medium that allowed this disjuncture a deceptive air of coherence.

The mobility of the image, and the moving body mobilizing the commodity of fashion, was mirrored in the march of production, epitomized by Taylorization and Henry Ford. The production line of bodies found its feminine equivalent in the stream of bodies made fluid by film. As Elizabeth Wissinger puts it: "Models led the way into a consumption-defined lifestyle by showing goods as a way to become part of the consuming community and, perhaps, win a chance to share the limelight."[48] The blurring of fashion shows in department stores and fashion houses and those recorded in films also had the effect of standardizing looks and gestures. By the 1930s, the complicity of fashion with Hollywood became a potent vehicle for consumerism, propagating a culture, as Wissinger states, "of luxury and glamour, expressed by objects made desirable by how they were portrayed in film."[49]

Although Doucet and Worth continued their dominance in such sumptuous *mises en scène*, at the time, they nonetheless experienced serious competition from, as Evans writes,

> Félix, Fred, Redfern, Wallès, Laferrière, Martial et Armand, Beer and Jenny, all houses that had large American sales.
>
> Many of them demonstrated a degree of stagecraft from the start. At Redfern the mannequins modelled beguiling gowns to clients in vast salerooms with soft carpets . . . Redfern, Paquin and Beer all had mirrored fitting rooms equipped with electricity for trying on stage costumes, a precedent set in the 1860s by Worth's *salon de lumière* brilliantly lit by hissing gas-jets with movable shades, in which customers could try out their ballgowns surrounded by mirrored walls on all sides. Both Beer and Paquin had modelling stages, an innovation of Lucile's that became a feature of many Parisian and a few American firms.[50]

Lucile was arguably the first designer to grasp the possibilities of the stage-like arena on which to place her highly trained mannequins. In 1925, in her Rose Room in Chicago, the models were presented in small alcoves framed with ornate curtains unmistakably connoting a miniature stage. It was a trend that, although not universally grasped, did begin to have a following. Paquin had a veritable stage rivalling any cabaret, complete with footlights and strong electrical spots. "Paquin is said to have concluded some of her shows with a ballet performance with the dancers all dressed in white."[51] A complement to the spectacle of modern life—cafés, café-concerts, salons, promenades, garden parties, terrace soirées—the judgment, experience, and consumption of fashion was not limited to the prospective consumer, but part of a greater pageant. People shared in the pleasures of consumption, of escapism, and of projection of who they could be. In her 1914 tour of the US, Paquin presented her models within a theatrical proscenium, with the audience seated in rows, with two aisles on either side. It was also not uncommon at this time for orchestras to play during fashion shows in department stores.[52] To present her collection in 1927, Vionnet had a shining arched portal designed by Lalique, where the models appeared, as if celestial visitors descending to earth.

The domesticated theatrics of Lucile

Although today much historical attention has centered on Chanel and Schiaparelli, the female couturier who preceded them, and who was the first female fashion magnate, was Lady Duff Gordon, aka Lucile. By the outbreak of war in 1915, the Maison Lucile and Lucile Ltd. was a multi-million-dollar company, and the first of any to have houses in London, New York, Chicago, as well as Paris, which opened between 1910 and 1915. Lucile knew from the first that fashion did not lie in the garment alone, and she brought her gifts for theatrical design and interior decoration together with the appreciation of photographic reproduction to turn her fashion into something more like a vision, or a culture unto itself. She would call on history, literature, the arts, and anything else that could evoke in her audience and prospective clientele the right need to partake in the same fantasy. Just as Worth before her plundered art history indiscriminately and arbitrarily to suit his own ends, Lucile would mine historical culture. One ensemble was named "Red Mouth of Venomous Flower," after Charles Algernon Swinburne's lubricious poem 'Dolores'" (1866). The beautiful young mannequins that she called upon to pose for these creations were in turn given pseudonyms like stage names. As Samantha Safer explains, Lucile conferred on her models names like "Dolores," "Hebe," "Gamela," "Florence," and "Phyllis," drawn from literature or mythology and supposed to correspond with each girl's personality.[53]

Giving the models sobriquets according to their disposition was also applied to classifying different interiors according to character or mood. Each room in her couture house carried a different theme, and in this respect resembled, but of course with deference to decorum, a brothel. In a redirected deference to the way sumptuous interiors can stoke desire, Lucile worked by the principle that a pleasing interior in which to show fashion was conducive to greater consumption. As she herself noted, one cannot "over estimate the effect of environment on a woman, for women are infinitely more adaptable than men, they become part of their surroundings."[54] A contentious statement for us now, and one very much of its time, Lucile knew the lengths that women would go to to be part of their surroundings, and do so in a way that would make their efforts evident, by wearing clothes that were of the same standard as the interiors they inhabited. And even a cursory survey of the literature dating from the nineteenth century onward makes womanhood—that is, largely middle- and upper-class womanhood—indivisible from, or interchangeable with, the domestic interior. Safer suggests that Lucile offered what couturiers at the end of the nineteenth century did not, which was to emulate in her interiors the homes of her clientele. Safer observes that "Even the great couture houses of the *fin de siècle* in or near the rue de la Paix, Paris [the same street where Worth opened his house], were not designed to resemble ladies' private spaces: they were more utilitarian than luxurious salons."[55] Worth had indeed been the first in the 1880s to make interior decoration a component of consumption, lining the walls in satin and lighting the rooms in low gaslight in anticipation of the same ballroom ambience wherein the gown would eventually be seen. But Worth's vision was decidedly public, not private. This changed in around 1910 when, as Safer states,

> interior design in the couture house drastically changed with Jacque [sic] Doucet, Jeanne Paquin and Paul Poiret taking their inspiration from the success of Lucile Ltd houses. In 1912 *Vogue* commented that while it was common practice to combine the sale of millinery, belts, caps and other apparel accessories, "certainly couturiers have never before insisted that chairs, curtains, rugs and wall-coverings should be considered in the choosing of a dress, or rather that the style of dress should influence the interior decorations of a home".[56]

This went so far that Lucile's fashion house in London, at 17 Hanover Square, resembled a stately private home. She would also encourage her clients to conduct their leisure time in there, with drawing room or salon-like spaces where they could play cards, relax, and take beverages.

One recurring room theme in her houses was the Rose Room, designed for choosing and fitting lingerie. If there be any critical doubt about the analogy to a brothel, then the "Pink Room" dispelled all doubt. It was a riot of scarlets and puces, with rose floral motifs and themes in the upholstery, and a replica of a day bed owned by Louis XV's famous mistress Madame de Pompadour. At the end of the room was a dressing table holding bottles of perfume, over which hung a gilt mirror with large lamps on either side. The window frames were adorned with rich swathes of fabric that called to mind stage settings.[57] One of the key designers for Lucile's interiors was Elsie de Wolfe, who in 1913 wrote an influential book on interior decoration, *The House in Good Taste*. Here, de Wolfe defended the aesthetics of eighteenth-century France because it was, as Penny Sparke affirms, "in the context of the early twentieth century, considered both modern and capable of extensive reproduction."[58] Moreover, the Louis XV theme was also an obvious choice for Lucile's ersatz boudoir, not only because of its close historical connection to sexual decadence, but also for the fact that the Rococo aesthetic, which had been much maligned in the revolutionary periods of the first half of the nineteenth century, was in the *Belle Époque* enjoying a widespread revival. From the late 1850s until 1878, the Goncourt brothers wrote four influential works on French eighteenth-century art and culture,[59] while the florid style of French Art Nouveau was in many respects a hybrid reinterpretation of Chinese and Japanese decorative art seen through a Rococo lens. Meditating on Art Nouveau as a phenomenon of turn-of-the-century subjectivity, Benjamin asserts that it was an expression of inwardness and the cult of personality: "In Vandervelde [one of the great Art Nouveau interior decorators] the house appears as the expression of subjectivity. Ornament is to this house what the signature is to painting."[60] These words have more than a little resonance with the developments of the presentation of early modern fashion. Under Lucile's influence, Poiret, Doucet, and others would play down some Baroque suggestiveness, adopting the more classical, linear, but still luxurious Louis XVI style. But in every case, lavish and imaginatively styled interiors made no ambiguity of the couturier's sense of intent, which was not only to assure the client's status and importance through luxury, but also through the illusion or reality of emphasizing her "unique" personality.

It is worth concluding this section with a few observations on Elsie de Wolfe, and her influence. In many ways, her *House in Good Taste* represents the first modern treatise on interior decoration, and in more than one way. Like modern fashion, de Wolfe emphasized how tasteful and beautiful homes were conducive to well-being, they were also signs of conspicuous consumption, and were vehicles for socially upward mobility. On a more lofty level, as Sparke writes, they afforded "the possibility of achieving a new level of self-knowledge and individualism, whether realized or fantasized."[61] Just as subtly and elusively, the book also revealed the tenuous balance of "real" and "ideal" in the representation of the tasteful interior. De Wolfe presented models as realities, which proved immensely popular.[62] This tension ran in close parallel in fashion photography at the very same time, which presented an anterior, idealized world as if it were the real one, whereby the fashion scenario and image became proposals, benchmarks for how to undertake a better life.

From Poiret to Rubenstein

Poiret was acutely aware of the benefits that accrued to the way in which early couturiers like Worth and later Lucile would freight their garments with countless material and immaterial trappings in order to give their collections a status on par with art. Lucile, for instance, was fond of extravagant titles that tipped into affectation, such as "Passion's Thrall" and "Do You Love Me?,"[63] thereby laying the ground for the evocative titles for collections used up until the present day. What Poiret also derived from Lucile was a penchant for using aestheticized environments to show off the clothes, many of which were so studied and intricate that the question went begging as to which was a vehicle for which, garment or setting. Like Lucile, Poiret used a custom-designed miniature stage, and, in the words of Andrew Bolton, "he also used the gardens of his *hotel de couture* as backdrops for his fashion shows. Indeed, he seized upon the outdoor setting as an opportunity to film his mannequins in motion."[64] While these shows were reserved for an elite, while in America he used the public spaces of fashion stories to daring effect.

Perhaps the best-known example of the first pageant-scale theatricalizations of fashion was Paul Poiret's "Thousand and Second Night" party that occurred on June 24, 1911. While designers such as Lucile and Paquin showed a taste for self-conscious show, the still conventional way of showing fashion was a procession of models down a runway, a method that was also sympathetic to reproduction in film, a medium that served for wider international consumption of the event. Poiret's "party" broke with all accepted convention of the fashion show, blurring the line between model and audience, as all participants were expected to dress in clothes from his Persian-inspired collection. Poiret explains that the idea came to him after attending a Bal des Quat'z-arts, or "Four Arts Ball."[65] This was an annual event initiated by a professor at the École des Beaux-Arts, Henri Guillaume, in 1892, four arts representing the school's departments of architecture, sculpture, painting, and printmaking. Combining art students and other members of bohemia, these balls were known as modern-day Bacchanalia, and from 1900 onward the parties had a themed character, usually Grecian, and costumes were mandatory.

The guests first donned the clothing supplied by Poiret, then were ushered into a room before which a "semi-naked negro draped in Boukhara silks, armed with a torch and a yatagan [a Turkish sword]" stood guard.[66] Visitors entered into what "called to mind a sun-filled patio belonging to Aladdin" with fountains and large bolts of vellum in blue and gold. Mounting several steps, the guests found themselves standing in front of a "huge golden cage, gilded with twirly ironwork" which held Mme Poiret, surrounded by a coterie of women "singing Persian airs." She was the queen of the harem, and her entourage the "ladies of honor." From there, one entered into a room with a spring that seemed to come from the carpet and which fell into an "iridescent crystal basin." Thereafter, through double doors, visitors came to a mound of embroidered cushions, at the summit of which crouched the celebrated actor Édouard de Max. He was dressed in a black silk gandoura (a long sleeveless tunic of Berber origin, typical to north-west Africa), and a necklace of "countless pearls." He was reciting stories taken from *The Thousand and One Nights*, with "one finger raised in the air in a gesture in homage to oriental storytellers."[67] An immense awning of over two hundred square meters hung over the splendor, painted by Raoul Dufy.

Departing this tableau, the room gave way to an "obscure and mysterious garden" where

> Carpets covered the tiles on the steps and the sand of the pathways, so that the sound of footsteps was muffled, creating a grand silence. Impressed by it, the people who strolled through it spoke in lowered voices as if in a mosque. In the middle of embroidered flower-beds was a vase made of white cornelian as stated in the program. The muted light through the branches around it gave it a strange illumination. Issuing from it was a thin spray of water similar to those found in Persian illustrations, while pink ibises wandered all around partaking of the freshness and light. Some of the trees were covered by fruit of a luminous dark blue; others had bays of violet light. Live monkeys, macaws and parrots animated all the greenery that seemed to be an entrance to a deep park. I was perceptible at the end, looking like a tanned sultan with a white beard, holding an ivory whip.[68]

Poiret, self-styled as Sultan Suleiman the Magnificent, was clothed in caftan trimmed with fur, tied with a green sash, large turban and slippers encrusted with gems. He too was surrounded by a small crowd of young women, his "concubines."[69] Once his three hundred guests had all entered, Poiret made his way to the cage, letting out his "favorite." She took flight "as would a bird," to which Poiret took pursuit, cracking his whip. After the grand opening, a concealed orchestra sounded in the distance in dedication to a "night of inebriation."[70]

This was more than some orgiastic conceit; it firmly placed Poiret's creations into the realm of eroticized Orientalist fantasy, with him as the uncontested leader modeled on the venerable Western vision of the Oriental despot. Always conscious of the shadow cast by Worth onto his own generation, Poiret choreographed his own fashion pleasure dome to eclipse all others. On a more practical level, it was also a celebration of movement and activity, themes that Poiret had a large part in introducing when he jettisoned the corset and introduced the *jupe-culotte*, or "harem pantaloons," essentially bloomers but without the associated conservative stigma. Poiret's inspiration came after the translation in 1899 of *The Thousand and One Nights* by J.-C. Mardrus, whom Poiret knew personally, a tour of North Africa in 1910, but above all following the triumph of Diaghilev's Ballets Russes after their interpretation of Rimsky-Korsakoff's symphonic poem *Scheherazade* in the same year. The Ballets Russes would have an almost hypnotic hold on theater, dance, music, fashion, and art until Diaghilev's death in 1929. It united many artists and fashion designers including Chanel and Picasso. To return to Poiret, while his 1911 party would never be surpassed, his talent for putting fashion on sumptuous display, and placing fashion within the ambit of other pleasures of the flesh, found another memorable example after World War I in his contribution to the 1925 Exhibition of Decorative Arts. For this, in the words of Peter Wollen,

> he placed three elaborate show-barges on the Seine, one for fashions, one for interior design and perfume, the third a floating restaurant. They were named *Amours*, *Délices* and *Orgues*, the three words in the French language that are of masculine gender in the singular, but feminine in the plural.[71]

To the present day, placing fashion against other constituents would continue to yield many unforeseen outcomes for reflecting on gender, sexuality, and identity.

It would seem unconventional, perhaps jarring, to place the work of Helena Rubenstein alongside Poiret, not least for the fact that Rubenstein was not strictly a fashion designer. But both had a preternatural knack for self-promotion and marketing, knowing that the success of commodities was not limited to quality alone. They knew that fashion and cosmetics were commodities that particularly lent themselves to aggrandizement, being easy devices for persuasion. They both had a developed feeling for theater, an inclination that saw them both drawn to and involved in the Ballets Russes.

In her detailed essay on Rubenstein, Marie Clifford opens with a description of a series of photographs that were published in an issue of *Vogue* in 1941, notable for their settings:

> An exaggerated, almost hyperbolic emphasis on decorative vocabularies coded as "feminine" creates a scene that hovers between lush fairyland and Technicolor™ movie set. One model occupies a room awash in shades of mauve and yellow, a pattern that extends to the walls, carpet and sculpted cherub. Bright pink curtains are reflected in strategically placed mirrors, and rows of yellow and white opaline glass complement the chairs painted in the same shades.[72]

This was far from Orientalist, but it does recreate a fantasy of ideal proportions filtered from, but barely belonging to, this world. A pale blue chandelier hangs from the ceiling, and the "wall resembles a display case and includes an ornate decorative relief of stylized floral patterns, bows and ribbons."

Rubenstein was an émigré from Poland who, after beginning her cosmetics business in Melbourne, moved to London and Paris and then to New York in 1915 as a result of the war. She was already a famous businesswoman in 1905, and her gift for marketing saw her amassing a considerable fortune, which was also used to invest in art. Rubenstein, whose chief competitor was Elizabeth Arden, had a keen intuition for how much could be woven around a commodity such as cosmetics, anticipating the suggestive industry of representations that drives the cosmetics and perfume industries today. Her shops were made to look like a combination of a lavish fashionable salon and a traditional apothecary, mixing luxury and culture with the image of serious scientific traditions. And her employees were scrupulously dressed in uniforms, bringing the language of the laboratory into the boutique. Her products were packaged with studied care that suggested luxury, and the products themselves were overpriced as an assurance to the buyer of the quality of the ingredients. If there were any room for doubt, the products were all endorsed by celebrities. She was the first to understand the power of suggestion that could be woven around cosmetics, and especially the ease with which a product can be assigned an *a posteriori* value. In other words, the consumer will search for and finally see the qualities invoked in the name of the product. Indeed, the product was but a vehicle for the consumption of an image, circumstance, or condition that in most cases was impossible to achieve.

The 1941 *Vogue* photoshoot described above marked the opening of her new line of shops in New York. Rubenstein had recently been married to Prince Artchil Gourielli-Tchkonia who said he was a Georgian royal. Authenticity was never Rubenstein's concern, only image: she was able to call herself "Princess" and to call her new salon "Gourielli's" after her husband's grandmother who was legitimately Princess Gourielli. Her salon, or apothecary boutique, had themed rooms such as the "Herb Room" or the "Gift Room," and these were elaborately decked out, not only in the most expensive materials and fittings, but also items from what by then was Rubenstein's vast personal collection of paintings. These were accented with colonial American antiques and glassware. The lavish spread in *Vogue* was an unashamed exercise in self-promotion.[73]

One of the chief sources of inspiration for Rubenstein's new rooms came from her recent experience of the Ballets Russes, on a suggestion from her husband. Rubenstein in her autobiography records how striking the colors of the production were and the effect it had on her:

> Accustomed as I was to the sweet-pea pastel stage sets of the times, the electric combinations of purple and magenta, orange and yellow, black and gold, excited me beyond measure! Warm, passionate colors, they were as far removed from my virginal whites and noncommittal greens as anything could be. . . . After the ballet, late as it was, I went straight back to the salon and tore down my white brocade curtains.[74]

The Ballets Russes were a catalyst for Rubenstein, who had hitherto treated the clothing and décor as components that did not compete with her products. But now they were all complements to the extent that they were part of the product itself. And her salon, as Clifford maintains, "became a space that acted on the body, transforming clients in ways that exceeded a simple makeover."[75] She argues that the salons at the very beginning of the century admitted of a "natural" body, whereas Rubenstein's new salons reflected a need to fashion and mold the body as a modern entity.[76] Furthermore, her emphasis on interior decoration complemented her business activities as a cosmetician, given that these had always been deemed the province of femininity.

And one of the biggest influences on Rubenstein was Poiret. The American fashion and design market took its lead from European taste, which is what she replicated in her salons. She was well aware of the way that Poiret made his own home into a place for showing off his own designs, complete with *objets d'art* and paintings. In the early 1930s, Rubenstein had even employed Poiret's interior decorator, Louis Süe, for the renovation of her own private apartment in Paris. Clifford remarks that the 1920s saw a number of fashion designers branch into interior decoration, including Lanvin, Schiaparelli, Champcommunal, and Vionnet. "As evidenced by a 1932 *Fortune* profile of Parisian couturiers, by the end of the 1920s, each French fashion house arranged itself as a kind of consumer product, 'selling' distinctive settings for the display of art and furnishings alongside the latest mode."[77] Rubenstein's American market was enthusiastic to see fashion incorporated into a larger composite of art and design, whose registers of modernism were unmistakable. Despite efforts by rivals such as Arden to eclipse her, Rubenstein proved highly adept at putting "good taste" on a stage. Her interiors were fantasies of domesticity. "'Domesticity'", Clifford continues, "itself became entertainment. One floor of the beauty parlor in her store at 715 Fifth Avenue was devoted to miniature dollhouses." These were dioramas with their own discrete historical theme, "and they linked Rubenstein's salon to current trends in fashion display."[78] The doll and the uncanny miniature were also a nod to Rubenstein's many artistic affiliations, in this case to her friendship with Man Ray and other Surrealists. Given the extent of Rubenstein's involvement with art and artists—collecting, patronizing, befriending, even acquiring African masks— she was to meld artistic display and fashion display on an unprecedented level. Making art seamless with fashion and commercialization raised many anxieties, but it also afforded many insights into the interrelationship of art and fashion, particularly in the potential of art to bring not only prestige but depth of meaning to the products displayed and sold. Hers is a signal example of what would continue to be exploited by designers and fashion houses to the present day.

Elsa Sciaparelli and the performative body

Poiret's cannibalizing of the art students' Saturnalia for the sake of fashion stirred many imaginations. Although the excesses that it celebrated experienced a lull in the wartime period, which valued thrift over profligacy (a turn that Chanel would exploit), the 1920s would return to the spirit of hedonism with convulsive force. The new modern, mobile body that Poiret helped to invent by abandoning the corset, followed by Chanel's and Patou's encouragement of the connection between fashion and sport, ushered in a new era of experimentation and cross-pollination.

It is telling, and unsurprising, that Schiaparelli's earliest forays into fashion were instigated by, and entailed, a considerable degree of performativity. Well before she had considered herself a fashion designer, in the years before World War I, she was invited to a ball in Paris by a family friend. At this time, as Poiret had freely exploited, the great sartorial inspiration had come from Bakst's vivid and motley designs for the Ballets Russes, and the pre-war hedonistic spirit of Orientalism hung in the air. With her instinct for invention and improvisation, Schiaparelli bought four yards of an expensive, heavy deep-blue crêpe de chine. An early form of what would become one of her signature designs, the bound dress without a single seam, Schiaparelli draped the dress around her body, also between her legs for what she called a "zouave effect."[79] It was all fastened by pins, and finished with a brilliant orange sash, as color complement to the blue.

As is well known, Schiaparelli began her career in the midst of artists and their circle, including Man Ray, Francis Picabia, and Guillaume Apollinaire. Her affinity with art was not only personal, but osmotic. This also helps to explain her lateral and frequently unconventional approach to fashion design. Like artworks, many designs can be read as solutions to problems, and as raising new questions. In the wake of Poiret, Schiaparelli's designs, culminating in her collaboration with Dalì, lent a particularly graphic, performative quality to the way that fashion is worn, effectively amplifying the relationship between display and wearing. For items such as her shoe hat (despite its short life), or the lobster dress, tend to eclipse the wearer and place him or her into an imaginary and theatricalized world that also creates a sharp contrast between such singular garments and the more conventional world around them. It is in the dramatic contrast and the way in which the garment, as it were, "stages itself" that we can draw a genealogy between early modernist examples of art-fashion and later figures such as Leigh Bowery, who is a living artwork for whom clothing, costume, and masking are all central. Such performances command a space unto themselves that is separate from the catwalk.

In the nineteenth century, as class barriers were more discernible, to cause a stir in "making an entry" was to announce difference through dint of sheer excess, or Brummell-like, to assert an indifference to such excess in the name of elegance. But in the era after the Great War and that of the artistic avant-garde, to *épater les bourgeois* (stir the middle class), as Baudelaire put it, could be achieved in inventive and perverse ways. These interventions into society can retrospectively be understood as an early version of what would later be called *dérives* by the Situationists, to be discussed in the following chapter, albeit those by Schiaparelli were not motivated by any social ideology as such, but more acts of personal promotion.

But that does not make them not worth citing, and one example of the performative gestures at which fashion was at the center, bears this point out. In the early 1930s, Schiaparelli befriended Daisy Fellows, which Schiaparelli's biographer Meryle Secrest explains was "tantamount to becoming, in the nineteenth century, the person who whispered in the ear of Beau Brummell and told him what to wear."[80] Born into nobility, she showed all the confidence of privilege that nourished a talent for self-aggrandizement. "As with Elsa," observes Secrest, "some deep need of her psyche made her compulsively rebellious, which made her reactions all the more perverse."[81] She was inclined to turn up to weddings dressed in black, or to funerals in red. But what would have been social solecisms to many were sustained by Fellows, whose wealth and taste could not be discredited. For instance, her mansion was decorated by André Mare and Louis Süe. Süe, it will be remembered, had decorated for Poiret and would do so for Rubenstein. Fellows would later become the editor of *Harper's Bazaar*.

The Paris that Schiaparelli and Fellows inhabited in the 1930s seemed less afflicted by the Depression than the US, or less ostensibly so, since it was a place of lavish expenditure, consumption, and show. Poiret's translation of the bohemian arts' ball into haute couture was reprised at this time as a way to leverage social cachet. Masquerades were abundant, but the need to be memorable made these parties more outlandish. Artistic talents were often called upon, such as Jean Cocteau, a friend of Chanel, Schiaparelli, and most of the *beau monde* would often be invited to exercise broad-ranging skills in lending ideas for fêtes that would outdo previous ones.

Three occasions stand out at this time. One was the party given by Jean Patou in which, as Secrest writes, "everything was encased in silver. His garden was roofed for the occasion in silver, silver walls went up, and those trees and branches that were included in the décor similarly disappeared under flamboyant cascades of silver."[82] Not to be outdone, the former actress Elsie de Wolfe, aka Lady Mandl, threw a Gold Ball. This entailed redecorating her salon with gold cloth, covering tables with gold lamé, having gold ribbons around the napkins, and painting the Champagne bottles gold. Rivalling the previous two, in 1932 the grandniece of Pope Leo XIII, the Countess Pecci-Blunt, assisted by a half dozen male aristocrats, held the "Bal Blanc": all guests were mandated to wear white, as were the waiters and musicians. Some arrived in white wigs designed by Cocteau and Christian Bérard. The *patronne* was photographed by Man Ray. Pecci-Blunt may or may not have been amused that her Bal Blanc would be revived in 1995 in Montreal, Canada: a huge rave party to mark the Easter weekend that continues to this day.

Upon the death of Madeleine Chéruit in 1935, Schiaparelli seized the opportunity to acquire her rooms on the Place de Vendôme for her own production and sales. These were decorated by Jean-Michel Frank, who had designed her first room in the attic nearby on the rue de la Paix. Decoration was assisted by Alberto Giacometti, who made plaster columns that concealed lights. Ashtrays, also designed by Giacometti, were displayed on spiral columns. On the ground floor, Schiaparelli had what was arguably the first Parisian boutique, known as "Schiap." Here, she made available one of the earliest examples of ready-to-wear ranges, including swim suits, dressing gowns, belts, hats, knits, lingerie, and scarves, some of which were arranged on straw mannequins.[83] Giacometti's input reflected a side of Schiaparelli's style that Victoria Pass calls "strange glamour."[84] This was allied, she argues, to Breton's notion of "convulsive beauty." It was beauty which carried with it the capacity to shock. "Shock tactics were crucial to Schiaparelli's practice and her creation of convulsive beauty and strange glamour. Shock practically became a second signature for Schiaparelli in 1937 when she created her signature shade, shocking pink, and the perfume *Shocking*."[85] This perfume was not just intended to compliment and prettify but to intervene and seduce. The bottle, designed by Leonor Fini, was modeled on the torso of Mae West, and has been described as the "the first sex perfume."[86]

It would seem that Schiaparelli's designs, as well as accessories like perfume, were intended to enable the wearer to make a performative statement. They were to create a stir that, while they may not have replicated Schiaparelli or glamorous friends such as Daisy Fellows, they were certainly an echo of the same. This desire to shock and intervene deepens the understanding of Schiaparelli's deep immersion in Surrealism, which is often blandly cited as a collaboration (which occurred mainly from 1936 to 1939 and notably with Dalì), and a signal instance of the art–fashion crossover. Rather, her attraction and, indeed, contribution to the Surrealist movement, group, ethos—depending on how it is defined—needs to be viewed in the light of her own personality that immediately responded to the kinds of ruptures and disruptions that the Surrealists, at their best, wished to instigate. Only Schiaparelli transported these approaches into fashion, which until relatively recently has caused her to be viewed patronizingly by critics, as the lowlier because commercialized, with the socially sanctioned refashioning of the avant-garde—the avant-garde made palatable and marketable. But perhaps the reverse is the case; in their time, some of the creations for which she has become most famous, the shoe hat and the lobster dress, would be immortalized, the latter being worn by Wallis Simpson, photographed by Cecil Beaton. The lobster dress—the lobster was a symbol for Dalì of sexual desire, and Wallis was no angel—was one example of where the shock lay as much in humor as in embracing the bizarre, a combination at which Westwood would later excel. As Francine Prose eloquently states:

> Nor did she borrow the Surrealists' images, but, more importantly, she appears to have absorbed the humor and the spirit that animated their work. She discovered ingenious

ways of using trompe l'oeil in the service of fashion; her first popular success was a hand-knit sweater patterned with a deceptively convincing bow, and she designed a Greek-style gown painted to create the illusion of flowing pleats.[87]

While Schiaparelli excelled at clean lines and practical, inventive garments, a characteristic of her work was to turn things on their heads; not only reversible jackets but a reverse jacket, or fantastic sculptural buttons. The body was thus conceived as not something to be simply dressed but used as an agent for the display and life of the garment, required for the performance of the garment itself.

2
FASHION (ALMOST) WITHOUT BODIES

In the previous chapter, we dealt with the placement of the body within scenic elements of narrative and the commodity, beginning with the exhibitions in London and Paris from the middle of the nineteenth century into the early twentieth. A central component of the display of fashion was through the pavilion and the panorama. Such exhibitions, largely devoid of living bodies, were translated in various ways by department stores and by fashion designers, who increasingly identified that in the modern age the spectacle could no longer rely on the mannequin alone to bring fashion to life. Nor was it any longer possible to view the garment as something autonomous, in itself, but more as sitting within a modulating network of images, intentions, and associations that were essential to the fashion experience. The idea of the fashion experience, while preponderant in films of fashion catwalks since 1910 and the rise of the fashion shoot at roughly the same time, was also conveyed in the boutique. Unlike the department store, which even today has niches, sections, and annexes devoted to particular brands and designers, the boutique acts as a kind of shrine or haven that expresses the fashion designer's sensibility, seen across a career or according to a specific collection at any given time. It was also the fashion boutique that influenced museological conventions of fashion display as they grew in the latter half of the twentieth century. This was already presaged in the work of the designers discussed in Chapter 1—and the genealogy of fashion installation that we trace has as many overlaps as it has abrupt divisions—from Lucile's stages to Rubenstein's salons. But apart from the extent to which these sites present the garment and body in a lavish and rarified context, they still bore resemblance to an interior, or a theater, however mannered and studied in their respective variations. The rise of popular culture and subcultures from the 1950s onward recast the meaning of glamor and desirability. In turn, fashion—the garment, the idea, the experience—found itself in places and purveying meanings that would have been anathema a few decades before. This meant that the spaces and semantics of fashion expanded exponentially. And the way it was displayed, the contexts in which it was delivered, both materially and conceptually, played a central part in defining its role in social and personal identity.

McLaren and Westwood

Perhaps the best place to start is with the series of shops ("boutique" in their case has a singularly ginger and precious ring that is incongruous for them) on 430 King's Road in London that launched the careers of Malcolm McLaren and Vivienne Westwood.[1] These shops, emporiums to mods, punks, bohos, and queers, existed under a number of incarnations, each of which bore a different name. The first was "Paradise Garage" whose look had a South Pacific air. This was followed by "Let It Rock," which opened in 1971. Steven Jones, who would later be a member of the Sex Pistols, commented that it was unusual, like being "in a shop but to hang out."[2] In the words of Westwood's biographer Ian Kelly:

> The front part of the shop, nearest the King's Road, was dominated by Odeon wallpaper, pictures of Billy Fury and Screaming Lord Sutch, and a suburban fifties display cabinet customized by Vivienne with pink taffeta and displaying Brylcream and paste earrings that might or might not be on sale. The whole deal was a mixture of vintage and reconstructions, in terms of the clothes and the décor.[3]

In its aesthetic, approach, and audience, this was all a far remove from the exquisiteness and excess of Rubenstein or Lanvin. Rather, McLaren and Westwood's shops and the things they contained were important historical markers in the approach to DIY design. The walls were papered with ripped fragments from 1950s soft pornography. To go with the look, Westwood bleached her hair and spiked it upward. With a rather rigid and operative class system in the United Kingdom of the 1970s, these kinds of clientele would not have felt comfortable in the traditional up-market couturier's house. "Let It Rock" was the subcultural alternative, or equivalent.

Subsequent transformations of the shop held the various names of "Sex" (or "SEX"), "Too Fast To Live Too Young To Die," and "Seditionaries." Miles Chapman remarks of "Seditionaries" that, "The white windows were so often smashed by soccer fans the front was boarded up, then sprayed by punks. Inside was an upside-down pic of Piccadilly Circus."[4] The shop presently endures as "Worlds End." Of her designs of the earlier years, Westwood states that she "made clothes that looked like ruins. I created something new by destroying the old. This wasn't fashion as commodity, this was fashion as idea."[5] "Fashion as idea," as Westwood calls it, would later be known in more official and recent design theory as "conceptual fashion" which would draw from conceptual art, of which installation practice was an essential component, and which we will discuss later in this chapter. What Westwood grasped at a very early stage is that garments could work symbiotically against one another and against objects and images that were read as belonging to the same semantic, ethical, aesthetic, and more broadly, economic family. These interrelations were in close synchrony with the way in which subcultures, as they emerged and evolved in the post-war era, created alternative worlds in which clothing and dress were inseparable from body-styling, lifestyle, and their lived spaces.

This marriage of garment and boutique became a more evident and decisive configuration with the ensuing venture that was provocatively named "SEX." The merchandise almost entirely black, the shop had the look of a sado-masochistic parlor. In correspondence with the theme, Westwood wore purple make-up and clothing like leatherette trousers with stilettos. The great innovation of McLaren and Westwood's ventures in this period was due primarily to motivation. For their primary intention was not to sell, it was not to open business. Instead, fashion, all the related accessories, and the decking out of the shop itself, was simply a vehicle for social comment. McLaren, who had been present in May 1968 in Paris and traveled there regularly, had imbibed the spirit of Situationism, the movement that began in the late 1950s with figures such as Asgar Jorn and Guy Debord. Deriving from avant-garde movements such as Dada and Surrealism, Situationism was a particular interpretation of Marxism that sought to make interventions upon society to rupture dominant modalities of power. As Debord observes in his still celebrated *Society of the Spectacle*,[6] modern society had become increasingly alienated, people's desires and aims manipulated by capitalism. While not exclusively an artistic movement (noting also that the original formation of Surrealism was as a poetic movement, not one devoted to the visual arts), Situationism attracted many artists and poets. They were drawn to the methods of Situationism to perturb the status quo, known as *dérives* to enact *détournement*, a way of turning the measures of capitalism against it, using shock and destabilization to implement change. This had already begun in the progenitor movement to Situationism, known as Lettrism, which used language to subvert habitual opinion and the dominant order. Influenced (to what degree is still debatable) by McLaren, these principles were put into practice by Westwood, who readily appropriated words and images as she re-appropriated garments themselves, re-shaping them to make subversive comments about power, politics, and sexuality. The combination of fashion and Situationism was an easy one, since both practices were, and are, pre-eminently performative.

It is also by understanding Situationism that we can begin to understand McLaren and Westwood's shops. They were not static places for showing wares, but very much installations unto themselves, in which the viewer/visitor/client took an active part. The distribution of the objects for sale worked together with the protean nature of the interior itself. The idea of constant changeability helps to underscore the many names as well, which was not motivated according to what we would understand as the rejuvenation of a product—such as a "sport" line of a well-known scent, or Coca-Cola repackaging a low-calorie version "Life" with the ideologically loaded color of green—rather it was more as an artist reconfigures an idea in response to personal inclinations and outside stimuli. As Westwood affirms, "Malcolm and I changed the names and décor of the shop to suit the clothes as our ideas evolved."[7] The shops were not only havens for the people who visited them, but they were also what in curatorial language is called a "laboratory," a place of experimentation, in which the merchandise and the fabric within are the raw material. This was a challenging social proposition, especially as capitalism has evolved today, when designing high-end couture boutiques has become its own specific specialization, such that the visitor is very much made to feel separate. This being the case, it does not mean that the McLaren/Westwood shops were as slipshod or as unruly as the clientele they were inclined to attract. On the contrary, John Savage, in his examination of youth culture, notes that, "Each phase [of the shop] had been marked by a rare degree of research and attention to detail."[8] This was in no small part due to McLaren's studies at art school, and his longstanding interest in art history.[9]

Although not single-handedly, just as they were not the sole originators of punk style, McLaren and Westwood's stores were instrumental in drawing attention away from the department store. Incidentally, the 1970s was also the period of the early evolution of what today is commonly known as the experimental art space and "ARIs," artist-run initiatives, which were *ad hoc* and often temporary sites and spaces for installing art and holding performances. These were natural off-shoots of conceptual art, performance art, and installation, which at this time were all intent on challenging the commodity status of art and therefore, by extension, the large official institutions themselves, the museums, which were understandably viewed as the storehouses of convention and of treasures. In August 1973, the McAlpine Hotel in Manhattan held a "National Boutique Show" where several shops from the King's Road were invited to "exhibit." "It was a trade show by any other name," writes Ian Kelly, "but predicated on an awareness that boutiques were necessarily niche-market."[10] It was open acknowledgment of the autonomy of boutiques and their ability to influence tastes. While in New York, Westwood was able to visit the New York punk venue established in the East Village by Hilly Kristal at 315 Bowery. Both this and the King's Road shop were lovingly reproduced in the exhibition *Punk: Chaos and Culture*, at the Costume Institute of the Metropolitan Museum in 2013. They were recreated, as Kelly describes, "as if they were the twin studios of a great artist or the scene of some infamous act of violence. In a sense they were both."[11]

The final remodeling of 430 King's Road, under the name "Worlds End" [sic], consisted of a sloped floor in the manner of a pirate ship, in homage to Westwood's first catwalk collection, "Pirates" (Fall/Winter 1981). A clock on the exterior of the shop shows thirteen hours and the hands run backward. After a brief closure, it was re-opened in 1986. As Miles Chapman puts it, "The front is a miniature of a cuckoo-clock and back of a galleon… the steps lead up to a rickety old door. Inside, the floor slopes alarmingly."[12]

From bodiless to clothes to fake bodies: Viktor & Rolfe

In the earlier days of couture in the first decades of the twentieth century, besides needing talent, if one had the right connections it was relatively easy to get a first break. Hubert de Givenchy, for instance, in addition to his imposing appearance, was an aristocrat, which no doubt would have been a sweetener to Schiaparelli, for whom he worked for four years. But by the 1980s, with the corporatization of fashion houses and with fashion becoming its own discrete discipline in higher education, the fashion industry did not only involve clothes, cosmetics, and brands, but also a rising number of trained professionals. In the first half of the twentieth century, to advance oneself in the fashion industry was still to follow an artisanal line, and to be associated with design and manufacture in a house from the very beginning. However, simply by dint of population and competition, to break into the fashion industry is a daunting task. It is harder than to break into the art world on the simple grounds of economics: an artist can conceive of a work that may cost very little (such as a performance or video work), whereas the fledgling designer must invest in materials from the very beginning, and then there is the concern over venues, paying models, publicity, and so on.

In the attempt to subvert this problem, the team Viktor & Rolf (Viktor Horsting and Rolf Snoeren) turned to a solution that is the very quintessence of fashion installation. Fashion was displayed and conceived as a series of art installations and performative social interventions. After both graduating from the Arnhem Academy of Art and Design, they moved to Paris in 1993, settling in the cheaper twentieth arrondissement. Their first works were not so much collections but rather critical engagements with the fashion world, and their difficulties with penetrating it. It was in seeing the fashion world in Paris as a complicated and inscrutable system built on protocols and gateways that they were spurred to ask where the garment itself was situated. For they were quickly compelled to see that the clothing of "fashion" was simply a touchstone for a much more complex and larger array of relationships that were semantic and economic. Their early sense of displacement and disorientation helps to explain one of their earliest fashion works, the exhibition *L'Apparence du Vide* (the appearance of the void) held at the Galerie Patricia Dorfmann, Paris, in October

1995. This consisted of bodiless garments made of gold lamé that called to mind clown suits made of gift-wrapping. These were suspended by chains, and made to hover over a mass of clothes made of black organza, as if these were the dark nemeses of the sinister golden, disembodied angels above them. A wall text, in gold vinyl, listed some of the world's top models, which was then echoed by a sound work of children reciting these names, with classroom uniformity. It was an ambiguous invocation to the bodies that were absent, and who occupied the world that the artists had yet to penetrate. At this time, the exhibition of garments out of an anthropological or museological context was unconventional, especially in a single commercial gallery, yet the installation did receive some critical attention in both art and fashion circles.[13] Their choice to use installation in their commentary on their exclusion from the fashion world was more than guided by the expedient of limited funds and resources. For installation, by its very nature, registers its incompleteness in time and space, and is thus inclusive of absence and discontinuity. In dealing with their own exclusion from both mainstream and high-end fashion, Viktor & Rolf mounted a more far-reaching meta-commentary on the porousness of the fashion industry itself, a porousness that commodity and the spectacle are at pains to disavow.

The "work" for which they had received the greatest notice up until then was in the same year (1996) with *Viktor & Rolf Le Parfum*, an empty perfume bottle that could not be opened. The launch had all the same hype and fanfare as any regular luxury perfume from a commercial house: an aggressive marketing campaign, press releases, and luxury packaging. But there was no scent. A much-cited reference point for the empty perfume bottle is Duchamp's *Air de Paris* (also known as *40cc of Paris Air*) (1919),[14] a tear-like globe of glass. But to this may also be added a later example of the play of absences, Michael Craig-Martin's glass of water placed on a glass shelf situated above eye-level, entitled *An Oak Tree* (1973). It is something whose gratuitousness, together with the title, reaches to the level of the monumental.

The reader will remember how the previous chapter began with a description of Chanel spraying her perfume *No. 5* throughout her boutique, and the saturation of Thierry Mugler's boutique with *Angel*. Viktor & Rolf were making an emphatic statement of the ways in which the fashion world was built around the immaterial, around desire, whim, novelty, and a groundless promise of something to come, but which is never materially present. Starting with the ubiquity and finality of the name itself, *Le Parfum* was in many respects the pure perfume, the distillation of the perfume industry which rested in suggestion, as the accompanying blurb maintained: "The perfume can neither evaporate nor give off its scent, and will forever be a potential: pure promise."[15] Fulfilling the prophecy, and in fact "completing" the work, the *ersatz* perfume nonetheless sold out.

By the mid-1990s, when Viktor & Rolf launched their ruse, the perfume market, together with that for cosmetics, had swelled to enormous proportions. The exhibition that ensued, "Launch" (1996), which also featured the perfume, was a canny and profound statement on the establishment and safeguarding of fashion houses through perfume. For they were simply following in a long and established tradition whereby either companies began with a fragrance (*Joop!*, Tommy Hilfiger), or kept themselves afloat because of it—Chanel's great wealth came from her ten percent share of *No. 5* under the company governance of the Wildensteins, while Schiaparelli could continue to live a lavish life after World War II, despite the dwindling fortunes of her fashion empire, due to her fragrance *Shocking* and other branding exercises (products using her name). With the introduction of synthetic aldehydes, the prices of original essences could be substantially off-set. Keeping the prices as if the essences were used could make perfume an immensely profitable prospect. More profitable still, Viktor & Rolf's perfume cost nothing, while what it did share with other lines was that the costs of packaging and marketing outstripped the perfume itself. Perfume is also a marketer's dream, since the powers of evocation and association are extreme: a pleasant smell can be married to any celebrity or scenario. Because of this, Viktor & Rolf could be said to have brought the condition of modern perfume, that is, its indissolubility to the narrative experience and the commercial image, to its foregone conclusion. The void was the ontological essence of perfume itself, the distillation of perfume *per se* to its basest elements of imagination and desire. It was an unforeseen, audacious, but in retrospect completely understandable intervention on the perfume industry that drew attention to the pre-existent qualities of perfume as an instrument of the commodity market, and the very proof of Marx's gnomic statement that "all that is solid melts into air."

"Launch" opened at the Torch Gallery in Amsterdam in October 1996. This was a Lilliputian version of an actual, full-scale fashion show, with a scaled-down catwalk with maquettes in the manner of theater design models, a down-sized boutique, and a photographic studio. There was also a light box containing miniaturized perfume bottles, with a photograph for the campaign to sell the 250 actual-sized bottles (with their obvious reference to Chanel's perfumes) that sold for £200 each. As Bonnie English observes, Viktor & Rolf's actions highlighted how printed exposure and the increasing media-hype surrounding catwalk productions generates a greater value than the garments themselves, or even their simple representations.[16] As one of the duo said: "We created the ultimate goals that we wanted to achieve in Fashion (but were unable to). These miniatures represented some of the most emblematic situations in fashion [that] we wanted to become a reality."[17]

Following this, for their Fall/Winter collection Viktor & Rolf made flyers proclaiming "Viktor & Rolf on Strike," posting throughout Paris and sending them to fashion editors. If they were on strike, it was in the capacity of designers who had never produced a collection recognizable to the fashion world as such. As Caroline Evans comments of the collection-without-a-collection:

Such tactics suggested that the designers were well aware that fashion is the ultimate product that emphasizes consumption at the expense of production, making the latter invisible in classically Marxist fashion. Viktor & Rolf managed simultaneously to critique the industry and its spectacle yet to be part of them in an ironic and knowing way.[18]

The insider critiquing the inside has always been a dilemma of art and activism, but carried out in fashion, the dynamic seems to have been a little less agonistic. Their strategies fitted firmly within the tradition of the Situationist *dérives* forty years before, but also in the manner of institutional critique and dematerialized art, typically where artists advertise an exhibition with a title and no venue, or having nothing in a gallery except an address to a link to some virtual, or hypothetical, venue. A memorable example in this vein is Santiago Sierra's contribution to the Venice Biennale in 2003. Policed by uniformed guards, only visitors holding Spanish passports were allowed to enter, to find an empty shell of a space with the remnants from the previous installation.[19]

Dolls, and the accompanying dolls'-house aesthetic, have always featured prominently in Viktor & Rolf's work. They are the ultimate cipher that expresses the absence of a body by posing as a substitute, and they are one of the key points of reference in the consideration of the performative body, artificial or not. This conundrum of the body in performance, which is by its nature an unnatural because self-conscious state, was considered in the much-cited philosophical meditation "On Marionette Theatre" (1810) by the Romantic writer Heinrich von Kleist in which he jarringly proposes that the movements of marionettes are in fact imbued with more beauty and grace because they are unencumbered by the spiritual and physical frailties of human affectation.[20] To gloss briefly, the narrator meets a mysterious Herr C, who informs him that he finds the movements of puppets more elegant than those of humans, as their limbs betray a lightness that we cannot match. Unlike puppets, whose movements are pure, humans conflate their actions with doubt. These stirrings of consciousness, impulse, and will distract us from the task at hand. This is the inevitable, unfortunate symptom of having eaten from the Tree of Knowledge. Expelled from paradise, we amble the earth to search for opportunities and places for our redemption. We must somehow resolve this split between our aspiration and our accomplishments, but it is uncertain whether this is ever possible. The problems besetting humans, according to Kleist's tale, is that they hesitate, question, and therefore spoil affairs with their desire.[21]

For their very first staged show in 1993, the models mounted a pedestal and posed as living dolls.[22] Having made maquettes in "Launch," for Paris Fashion Week in 1998, Viktor & Rolf staged a performance for their "Babushka," or "Russian Doll," collection, where they treated the model Maggie Rizer as an insensate mannequin, heaping layer upon layer of highly styled couture garments one on top of the other, then undressed her, in reverse sequence. Even if in this case the body was present in the display of clothing, it was just as much undermined by treating it as an object. For their ready-to-wear collection of 2003, Viktor & Rolf, who had already gone to great lengths to make themselves look like twins, turned the doll theme on themselves, choreographing look-alikes to dress and undress on stage. As Snoeren himself states, the catwalk events are "not just about showing the clothes—they're performances."[23]

As we have already canvassed in the introduction, the role of the doll in fashion has an important and long history, but with the theme of fashion installation in mind, it is worth digressing to discuss an important event involving fashion dolls that occurred toward the end of World War II. With both materials and skilled labor in short supply, the fashion industry was at every level in disarray. After the liberation of Paris in August 1944, Raoul Dautry, a member of the aide agency Entr'Aide Française, proposed an initiative to revive what had been one of the most, if not the most, important tertiary industry. He approached Robert Ricci, son of Nina, in the Chambre Syndicale, the chief fashion body. The proposal was to make a series of fashion dolls and to insert them into the appropriate diorama, miniaturized stage settings. The bodies were wire frame (made by André Beaurepaire and Jean Saint-Martin), while the unpainted plaster heads were designed by the Catalan sculptor Joàn Rebull. All the principal couturiers were invited to design clothing for a number of dolls.

The artistic director, Christian "Bébé" Béraud, was a close affiliate of Schiaparelli, and other designers. He invited a number of his friends to design the stage settings for the dolls. These included painters, theater decorators, and designers, such as Jean Cocteau, Emilio Grau-Sala, Georges Geoffroy, Georges Wakhevitch, and the ballet impresario Boris Kochno. The clothes were representative of the Spring/Summer collection for 1945, and included seventy couturiers, who clad a total of two hundred and forty dolls. They were outfitted with consummate skill and an eye to detail, which meant not only to-scale clothing but likewise hair, hats, gloves, furs, handbags, jewelry, umbrellas, even zippers and buttons. Cartier and Van Cleef & Arpels supplied precious baby jewels. The results were so splendid that they carried an ambiguous message: a willingness to rebuild the future, but a melancholy over an irretrievable past. The exhibition opened in March 1945 at the Pavilion de Marsan in the Louvre, attracting over one hundred thousand visitors in only its first weeks. The dolls were then shown, with equal success, in London, Leeds, Barcelona, Copenhagen, Stockholm, and Vienna, then in New York and other cities in America in 1946. The exhibition was reprised in 1990 due to the efforts of the bureau chief of Condé Nast, Susan Train. The success of the enterprise owed itself to a number of factors, not limited to the designs and the skills in reproducing the dolls, but due to the disarming ease with which dolls can be looked at, as well as the settings provided by Cocteau, Kochno, and many others, offering the viewers charming and immersive vignettes of what Paris and the world could be again.[24]

To return to Viktor & Rolf, the doll, important as a trope from the very beginning of their careers, is now integrated into their collections in the most systematic way. Each collection is accompanied by a series of dolls, which, among other things, serve as an *aide mémoire*, and also as an ongoing solution to the dilemmas besetting the exhibition of fashion. For the duo, the dolls are a way of ensuring the timelessness of the fashion object, as Snoeren comments, "What appeals especially to us about these porcelain dolls, is that fashion is so disposable nowadays. It goes so fast. And it feels like we are freezing time by making all of these dolls."[25] Moreover, the dolls are artifacts that stand together with the artifact of haute couture. After all, many of their creations are so bold and intrusive that they would be difficult to wear, and so their critical and allegorical content is made to live on by the dolls, which, when seen as a larger corpus, afford a strong impression of the development of their designs over two decades. The dolls were first exhibited at the Barbican Gallery in London, and subsequently at the Royal Ontario Museum in June 2013, and at the National Gallery of Victoria in 2016. For the show at the Barbican, the dolls were placed in alcoves and interiors within a (miniaturely) gigantic, dolls' house structure.

In other comments about their devotion to dolls, Horsting and Snoeren admit to being drawn to the instinct for play that dolls suggest. Yet, the dolls are also a way of "taking control,"[26] as they are a sympathetic means of taking the measure of the growing corpus of their work, being a homogenizing armature that plays down hierarchies. As Snoeren continues, after ten years of work:

> We felt a strong need to do something that related to our old work, to use it and make it part of a new story, a bigger one, to turn it into something new—and also homogeneous maybe. By showing all of this together in a doll's house, as if it were one big projection of the future or better maybe, a retro-vision of the future, we try to edit our own past and put a spell on our fates. It was also clear to us from the start that we wanted to use the exhibition to create new work, outside of the context and conditions of the fashion system.[27]

This need to place a foot outside the fashion system should not be downplayed, especially when considering fashion installation and its open-endedness. Their dolls have a dual function of sanctifying their collection into timelessness, but at the same time, diminishing the pomp and circumstance that is so much of the official fashion catwalk. As objects for play, the dolls insert themselves both physically and psychologically into a lost or neighboring experience. The uncanny dolls stare at the spectator with innocence and indifference that is at once intimate to us from some distant childhood past, while also permanently frozen, foreign, and unfathomable. They are also yet another expression of the desire inherent to fashion, as they enshrine a desire that is intimate but also remote and unreachable, existing in a small mirror, a world not our own.

Concept boutiques and pop-up shops

Like conceptual fashion where the abstract, immaterial idea holds as much sway as the tangible garment, or where the garment exists for the sake of conveying an idea, the concept store contains a selection of products from different designers or brands that are carefully curated to connect to an overarching theme (or concept). More often than not, the themes usually evoke a lifestyle that is aspirational and is defined by customization, experience, personalization, community, and curation to appeal to a particular target consumer. Similarly, the concept store is intended as a space of discovery where the products or theme (story) change regularly to keep the concept fresh, much like a fashion installation. An important aspect of the concept store is that it usually contains experiential areas such as a café or restaurant, and it is intended as a space that builds a following or a community around the lifestyle that it embodies. Although not limited to fashion, the first high-end fashion concept store, 10 Corso Como in Milan, was conceived and established in 1991 by Carla Sozzani (editor of Italian *Vogue* and Italian *Elle*) (Figure 5). In 2002, 10 Corso Como opened in Tokyo in partnership with Rei Kawakubo and Comme des Garçons (as well as stores in Seoul, Shanghai, and Beijing), and most recently in 2017 in Lower Manhattan, New York. The concept store describes itself as a "multifunctional space, a meeting place, [a] union of culture and commerce"[28] and incorporates a gallery and exhibition space, a bookshop, a three-room hotel, a café, and restaurant.

On December 20, 2017, the famed boutique and concept store Colette in Paris closed for business. Established by Colette Rousseaux two decades previously, in 1997, on Paris's chic rue Saint-Honoré, Colette became synonymous with luxury fashion and associated with the lifestyle of the rich and famous. Known for its collaborative associations with Chanel, Hermès, Yves Saint Laurent, and Balenciaga, much like a pop-up shop that is "taken over" by a fashion brand, Colette was a curated mix of products that ranged from garments to street wear, magazines, gadgets, music, and art. Robert Burke, founder of Burke Consultancy, believes that

the selection of brands, the way the forms displayed, the clothes and the mix of designers was inspiring. If you were carried at Colette, you were cool. If you had a launch of product or a book signing at Colette you were recognized by not only the fashion world but the international fashion consumer.[29]

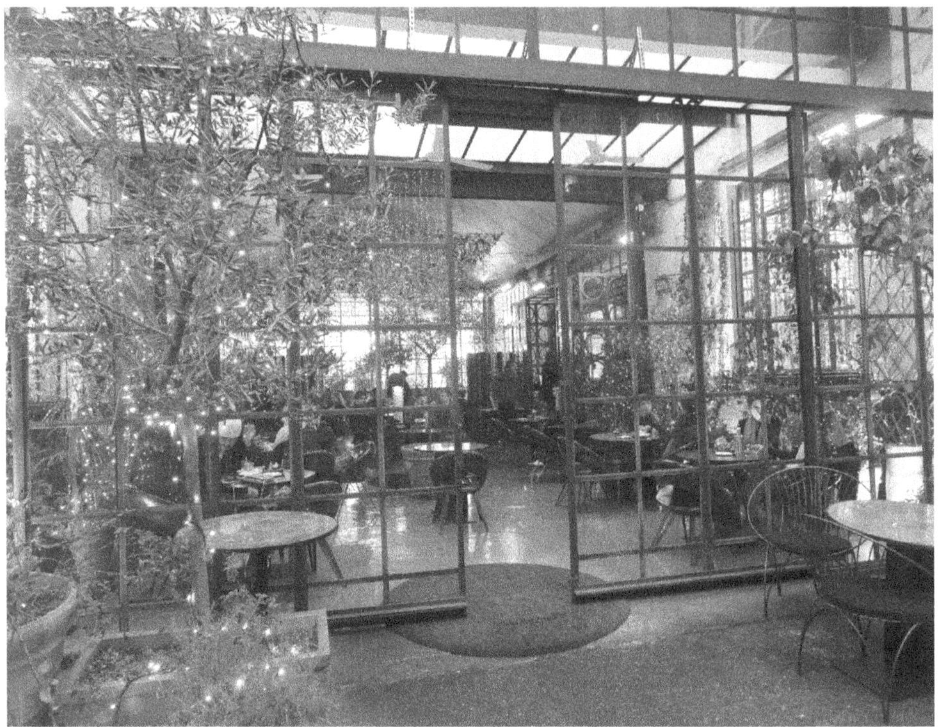

Figure 5 10 Corso Como store and gallery, Milan, Italy.

In 2017, Colette partnered with Balenciaga, who created exclusive pieces such as lighters, mugs, and sleeping masks as well as hoodies and sports trainers. In addition to the eclectic mix of products, Demna Gvasalia, Balenciaga's creative director, held a series of events during its six-week occupancy, which included installations and an art exhibition. On October 2, Thom Browne began a month-long residency at Colette when he transformed the store's second floor into an installation of his American office which included mid-century furnishings. Tattoo artist Leo Garvagio offered customers personalized Thom Browne tattoos, and Italian restaurant Sant Ambroeus opened a pop-up café providing homemade sweets. The three-story building contained a fashion boutique with high-end designer garments, a library, and an art gallery with new installations each month, as well as a water bar restaurant in the basement that offered over ninety brands of mineral waters.

In 2004, Rei Kawakubo, along with business and life partner Adrian Joffe, opened Dover Street Market (DSM) at 17–18 Dover Street, Mayfair (Figure 6). On the site of the

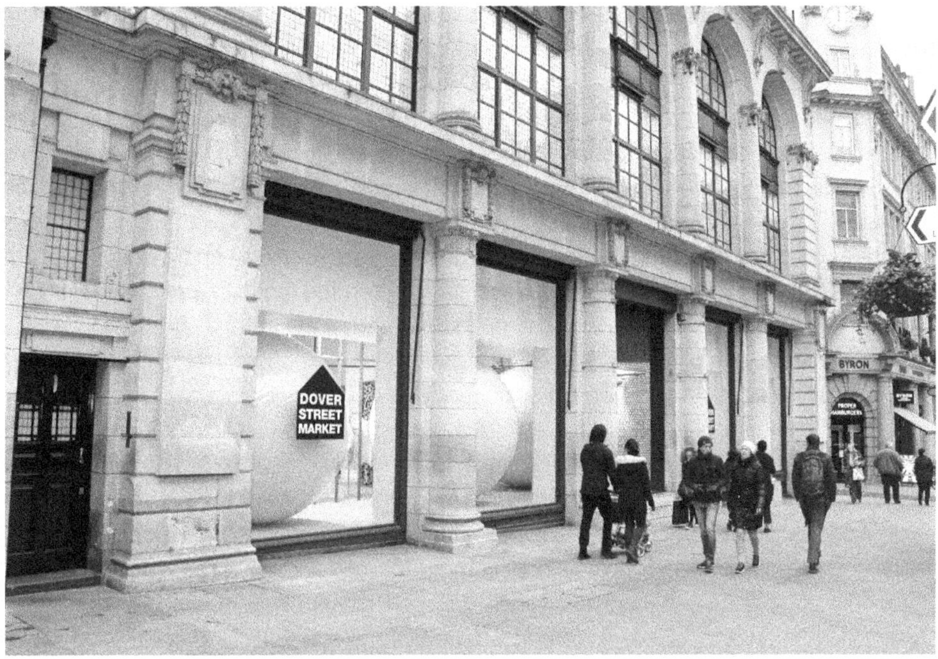

Figure 6 A general view of the atmosphere at an exclusive VIP preview of the Dover Street Market on March 18, 2016, London.

former Burberry Building erected in 1912, it also became the home of the Institute of Contemporary Arts (ICA). Later, in 2016, the concept boutique would be relocated to Haymarket, and stores were also opened in Ginza Tokyo, in Manhattan in the former New York School of Applied Design building (1908) on Lexington Street, in Singapore, and in Beijing. Plans and construction are also underway to open a DSM in the downtown arts district of Los Angeles. Considered more fashion installation than boutique, the concept store is curated by Rei Kawakubo and stocks the likes of Gosha Rubchinskiy and Vetements, as well as the more established labels Yves Saint Laurent, Gucci, Prada, and Burberry who maintain creative control over the layout of their collections. Described as "part high end shopping, part art museum, part trendy eatery,"[30] the Tokyo, London, and New York stores boast a Rose Café, and the Dover Street Market in New York contains seven floors that are reached by a glass elevator that is located in the center of the boutique. Like Colette, DSM stores maintain collaborations with designer brands that offer "drops" and "one-offs" so as to maintain exclusivity amongst its buyers. In 2017, Balenciaga opened its personalized T-shirt printing service in London's Dover Street

Market. First introduced during Balenciaga's takeover of the Colette concept store in Paris 2017, customers could create their own designs using a selection of Balenciaga logos and graphics. The text "Balenciaga Do It Yourself Ts" is featured on the back of the T-shirts. The London installation also featured a sculpture by artist Mark Jenkins and video screens. Similarly, Gucci launched its exclusive Gucci Cruise 2018 collection that was only available at Dover Street Market stores. The new range was part of a partnership between Dover Street Market and the Italian high-end fashion label and consisted of garments and accessories: tracksuits, bomber jackets, blazers, and T-shirts with the word "Guccified" in boldly printed graphics stamped on the fabric.

Pop-up stores, or flash retailing, has become a common strategy that fashion brands use to create consumer interest in their label, launch new products, test niche markets, or increase the "cool" factor. Pop-up stores occupy a space typically from one to three months and tend to favor high-traffic areas such as shopping malls or busy streets, and may also function as promotional events to increase brand awareness. Borrowed from art and arguably perfected by fashion, pop-ups were art events that originally were solutions to the lack of permanent gallery space or specific art venues. In warehouses or shops in between leases, or in more official venues such as community halls and the like, artists would stage temporary exhibitions and accompany them with performance events, which would then be dismantled as quickly as they were erected. Pop-ups are exhibition as celebration, which makes them more than conducive to the fashion world that now regularly commissions contemporary artists as curators or stage-managers. Pop-up shops offer consumers lower-priced goods, such as scarves, perfumes, or make-up, and are geared to entice a younger clientele who have lower shopping budgets. In this way, a brand can introduce itself to a different generation of consumers who, over time, will become loyal customers.

Take the Paris-based luxury fashion label Hermès, which recently opened a series of pop-up stores in London, Hong Kong, and across the United States. In 2015, Hermès opened a pop-up shop at John F. Kennedy Airport Terminal 4 (JFK) that was modeled on the brand's flagship store in Paris and sold scarves, home goods, and perfumes. This, however, was not the brand's first foray into flash retailing; following in the footsteps of the London "Silk Bar," Hermès had opened a pop-up showroom in Hong Kong in 2009 that was built in a converted shipping container that moved between two locations. Scarves and accessories were on display, while drinks were served to customers and a disc jockey played an upbeat playlist. In 2013, the company hosted a pop-up shop in Grand Central Station Terminal, then the following year the "Silk Bar" opened at 10 Columbus Circle in a classic American diner. Upstairs, there was an augmented reality (AR) environment implemented to coexist with the physical products on display and to enhance the consumers' shopping experience. A roll-over video screen revealed the historical connections associated with the scarves' patterns which were first made in 1937, as well as the "Hermès Silk Knots" computer application (app) with tutorials and workshops on how to tie a scarf. Two levels up from the Silk Bar was Les Jeux d'Hermès (the Games of Hermès) where customers were invited to jump ropes, play with hula-hoops, and have a game of mini-golf. Hermès' latest (and final) pop-up venture was the "Hermèsmatic" laundromat and dip-dye concept store in Los Angeles. The interactive installation offered consumers the opportunity to "breathe new life" into their existing worn scarfs by using a dip-dye washing technique as well as the chance to purchase an exclusive (and limited) scarf from the Hermès dip-dye collection. "The idea of the pop-up is to 'surprise' our existing and future clients by encountering Hermès in a totally unexpected location, and in a very unexpected way,"[31] said Robert Chavez, chief executive officer of Hermès USA. From recycled shipping containers and laundromats, where people of all walks of life are thrust together, to classic retro American diners, the Hermès pop-up store installations are intended to transport the consumer to a time and a place that represent the brand's core values and principles of heritage and tradition. Hong Kong was founded as a shipping port and colonial trading outpost of the British Empire, and the humble American diner is an icon of American culture with its chrome counter, formica table top, cherry pie, burgers, and cups of joe (coffee), symbols of honesty, hard work, and opportunity embodied in the American dream. In short, the sites and concepts of the Hermès fashion installations were chosen because of their association with heritage (Hermès began trading as a saddlery and a supplier of equestrian leather goods in 1837) and its connection to the "good times" and physical artifacts and tangible attributes from the past into the present. Heritage in fashion retailing is about creating a brand story, a unique narrative or myth about tradition or craftsmanship, or even the revival of an image.

Honor Thy Heritage: installing nostalgia and authenticity

Fashion brands (especially luxury brands) establish an identity by creating a particular narrative that will appeal to a targeted consumer. It is this mythology that is used in store installations to create an image associated with a lifestyle that is embodied by a product and extended to the consumer. The product and all its associated signs, imagined and lived, are embedded in the brand. "The brand," writes Patrizia Calefato, "in fact, is a sign bearing a special power sitting in between language, merchandise and values."[32] For Calefato, "brands not only have the function of designating a product in order to distinguish it from other products: they also incarnate a concept, a value, an emotion, a narration."[33] Calefato begins her analysis of the power of the fashion brand by examining the writings of the Hebrew mystic scholar Gershom Scholem and his research into the role of clothing in the multiple versions of the Kabbalistic manuscript *The Book of Clothes*, which was written before the Kabbalah was formed in the thirteenth century. Calefato refers to Scholem's research, which describes the process of wearing the secret names of God on a piece of parchment, which is then used in the design of a sleeveless jacket and hat. The mystic then wears these garments for seven days, avoiding anything impure, material or otherwise, whilst he shouts the name of God as an act of purification, which, as Scholem writes, is contained in the power bestowed on his name. Using the above analogy, Calefato proposes that the power that is invested in the name of God (a sign that can be translated) is represented by the brand. She takes Scholem's hypothesis one step further and uses the sign of God, which possesses multiple meanings and is a key concept in culture, to imagine the existence of a cipher in a modern world that unravels the connections between the text, the body, and culture. As Calefato observes, in the same way as the Kabbalistic mystics who wore the name of God sewn into the lining of their garments, so too do we wrap our bodies in clothes that contain names, brands, logos, signatures, and labels whose names (Gucci, Prada, etc.) contain multiple meanings bound to discourses of class, tradition, heritage, craftsmanship, and so on. Calefato comments that the "brand is a sign bearing a special power sitting in between language, merchandise and values. Brands not only have the function of designating a product in order to distinguish it from other products: they also incarnate a concept, a value, an emotion, a narration."[34]

For example, Westwood and McLaren's store on the King's Road in its various incarnations: it is associated with the concepts of rebellion and anarchy as well as working-class values. The interior of "Sex" contained graffiti scrawled on the walls, rubber curtains, and chicken wire; later, when the store was rebranded to "Worlds End," it underwent a refurbishment to resemble an old curiosity shop with a galleon and a cuckoo-clock that displayed thirteen hours and ran backwards. Once the home of rockers and punks, Worlds End invoked and courted chaos, the world turned upside down.

Taking Calefato's analogy still further, the high-end fashion brand is a sign that evokes the concept of luxury and denotes the social world of the idle rich and famous. A life made possible by the name of a designer, be it Karl Lagerfeld or Yves Saint Laurent, for example, that in contemporary times has replaced the name of God. Trawling through an internet search on luxury brands, one finds an exhaustive list of labels that have come to represent, both real and imagined, an "extraordinary" social world of extraordinary people who are extraordinarily beautiful with extraordinary bodies and who live extraordinary lives wearing extraordinary clothes and driving extraordinary cars.

Oh the lifestyle of the rich and the famous: imagine stopping by Tiffany and Co. on your way to lunch to pick out that perfect piece of luxurious jewelry, then spending the afternoon with friends at the Waldorf Astoria, followed by stopping by the Prada store to find that outfit to add to your ever-growing wardrobe, then ending the night at one of the famous Four Seasons Hotels. Of course all of this traveling happens in your beautiful Audi with your Louis Vuitton handbag lying on the passenger seat. We all daydream about living a life like this—a life full of luxurious comforts.[35]

Even further still, the heritage fashion brand not only contains all the above trappings associated with luxury, it also maintains a long tradition of quality products made by experienced artisans. Heritage brands evoke the concepts of nation, tradition, inheritance, authenticity, nostalgia for another place in another time. This brand image is not only communicated through media campaigns, but also through the stores' installations, which extend the brand's identity, what Otto Riewoldt refers to as "brandscaping."[36] Simply put, brandscaping is about creating landscapes or environments that present the brand image and the encounter with the product as an emotional experience of the senses. In other words, brands are now "commodifying" authenticity as their focus is no longer on the product, but on building associations with particular lifestyles by using installations to make an emotional connection with the consumer. The Hermès pop-up stores, for example, were not really designed to sell garments, but were intended for customers to experience and immerse themselves in the Hermès brand and to attract a younger generation who have grown up surrounded by the iconography of fashion brands.

The Come Back Kids: British heritage labels and all-American style

In creating an American mythology, Victoria Manlow remarks that "all fashion brands create an identity that will be meaningful and memorable and particularly American heritage brands." Tommy Hilfiger, Ralph Lauren, and cult brand Levi's rely on a particular myth of American democracy and freedom that is created and sustained in the location and design of in-store installations. Levi's has paid particular homage to the American myth of the taming of the wild frontier and its association to working-class values and the pioneering spirit. However, Levi's' historical references to Americanism and 1950s Western-style fashion fell short in the 1990s as youth street culture, with its associations with grunge style and the city, had eclipsed ideas of vintage and retro-styling, forcing the label to rebrand. Not only was the iconic jean "re-engineered" but its flagship stores on Regent Street, London, and Market Street, San Francisco, were redesigned into multimedia theme parks that reflected urban youth culture. The goal was to "create an environment where fashion, art, and music converge."[37] The London flagship store contained movable screens and walls that conveyed the impression of an exhibition space. A two-story cylinder tower contained a disc jockey (DJ) who played rave mixes behind a perforated steel screen that linked the ground floor and the basement with a "chill out" space much like in a nightclub. Other installations included computer terminals with internet access, video productions, temporary art installations, and book and music counters. In the "customization" area, customers could turn their newly purchased jeans (or ones brought in from home) into artworks by using laser etchings, dyes, or embroidery. In 2013, the San Francisco flagship moved its location and was redesigned but kept its exhibition space and displayed artwork from Bay Area artists. At the entrance of the store is an art installation by Peterson Neon of an American flag against a reclaimed wood wall, a neon sign reads, "The Future is Leaving." The flag associated the brand with preconceived ideas of what constitutes nation and ideas of Americana. As part of its 2016 "We Are 501" seasonal campaign, which highlights influential taste-makers and their 501 jeans, Levi's invited people of influence to create a "living, breathing mural" as part of its San Francisco store window. French fashion icon Caroline de Maigret, American DJ Classixx, and Chinese multimedia artists Yi Zhou participated in creating a curated video of what Levi's means to them, and then screened the video in the store window. The campaign was intended for consumers to participate by sharing their 501 experiences via the hashtags #501 and #LiveInLevis. The intention of the campaign was to produce images that reflect the aspirations of the brand and to identify Levi's with a creative pool of people that reflects the image of the company.

American heritage labels, like Levi's, Brooks Brothers, and Ralph Lauren, generally fall under gender archetypes; the collegiate East Coast preppy, the western cowboy and cowgirl, the socialite and successful entrepreneur. These archetypes play a major role in the curation of a retail space in their use of visual merchandise and installations. The Ralph Lauren (RL Corporation[38]) menswear flagship store in New York is a prime example of how the installation of a retail environment serves to highlight the brand's association with American archetypes and Old World charm and aristocracy. Lauren extracts and reconfigures ideologies of Americana, of individual freedom, hard work, and democracy, and truncates them into commercialized aspirations that can be purchased and consumed. As D. J. Huppatz and Manlow: "Success once reliant on hard work, or inherited wealth is made aspirational and immediately accessible, the old markers of elite heritage severed from a closed system and worn on one's sleeve" (quite literally).[39] Housed in the Revival château that sugar heiress Gertrude Rheinlander Waldo built for herself in 1898 on Madison Avenue at 72nd Street, the flagship store's architectural façade represents the brand's image. With its ornate wood carvings, winding mahogany staircases with oil paintings of Victorian and Edwardian gentlemen and stucco ceilings, each floor of the store is curated to represent each label; a gentlemen's club (Ralph Lauren Purple Label), an equestrian country polo club (Ralph Lauren Polo), a western outpost store (Ralph Lauren), a quintessential "playboys' den" with gadgets and even a rare Confederate 120 Fighter Combat handmade motorcycle (which can be purchased)—very James Bond—and the RLX sports brand with carbon-fiber racing bike designed by Brooklyn's Affinity Cycles exclusively for Ralph Lauren. Directly across the road is the Beaux Arts-style womenswear flagship store; like the menswear store, each floor is a dedicated curated space reflecting the brand's label and its association with upper-class luxury. Designed to match the menswear store, the Beaux Arts building boasts an Indiana limestone façade with black iron wood doors and window railings. The interior is curated to resemble an aristocrat's retreat that has been transformed into a turn-of-the-century shopping arcade with Turkish marble pillars, illuminated display cabinets, and jewel-box vitrines. Beveled mirrors and black-and-white photographs of nineteenth- and twentieth-century socialites hang on the stairwell, a collection that includes British prime minister Winston Churchill's mother, New York debutante Jennie Jerome, and a portrait of the 1970s music star Diana Ross painted by Victor Strebneski. The curated photographs are intended to evoke the glamor associated with high-society balls and a privileged life.

On the March 1997 cover of *Vanity Fair* magazine, the lead singer of grunge band Oasis Liam Gallagher and actress Patsy Kensit (soon to be married) were photographed by Lorenzo Agius sprawled on a Union Jack flag bedspread. The article, with all its accompanying "hep cat" jingoism of the 1950s Beat Generation, began like this:

> *Flicker … whirrr …* Move it along, Granddad, you're getting in the way of The Scene! The London Scene, that is! From Soho to Notting Hill, from Camberwell to Camden Town, the capital city of Dear Old Blighty pulses anew with the good vibrations of an epic-scale youth quake![40]

The quest for authenticity and nostalgia for the past comes no greater than the "Cool Britannia" campaign that was launched in Britain in 1996. Reminiscent of the cultural hub that was "Swinging London" in the 1960s, the campaign was intended to rekindle nostalgia and pride in all things British, especially art, fashion, and music (although it miserably failed). A press release issued by the then Tory Government's Department of National Heritage declared that "London is universally recognized as a center of style and innovation. Our fashion, music and culture are the envy of our European neighbors. This abundance of talent, together with our rich heritage, makes "Cool Britannia" an obvious choice for visitors from all over the world." This was the rebranding of Britain, and with it came an abundance of creativity: big money, hedonism, and acclaim. Considered by its European and Atlantic counterparts as stuffy and conservative, now all things young, cool, and cosmopolitan reigned supreme. It was all about Brit-Art, with Damien Hirst and the yBas (young British artists), and Britpop with Oasis and the Spice Girls. British cooking, with its perceived bland palate, became sexy under food-porn stars Jamie Oliver and Nigella Lawson, and fashion was ruled by the *enfants terribles* Vivienne Westwood, Alexander McQueen, and John Galliano. Whilst Westwood celebrated raunchy British humor in her "Anglomania" (Fall/Winter, 1993) and "Liberty" (Fall/Winter, 1994) collections, McQueen and Galliano plundered from the annals of British history and the glory days of Empire. The revival of British heritage labels Doc Martin, Fred Perry, Pringle, Acquascutum, and Burberry made traditional popular again, and British fashion came back in vogue. In the midst of all this explosion of cool, Paul Smith reinvented traditional tailoring and collaborated with British Rover Mini to design a limited-edition car in his pinstriped barcode of rainbow colors (Figure 7).

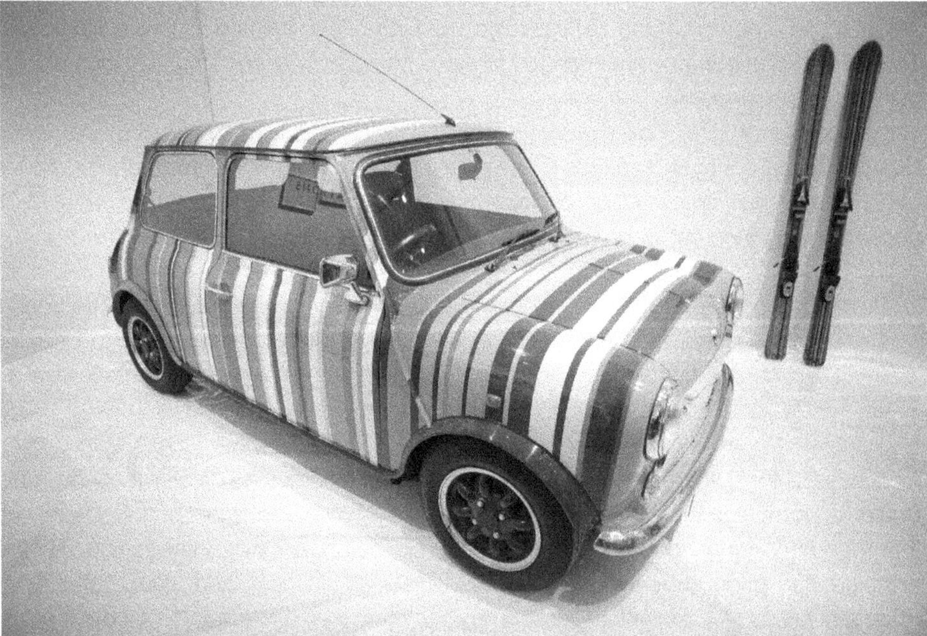

Figure 7 A Mini by fashion designer Paul Smith. Paul Smith's design was based on a fashion print he had created, and he said that "Paul Smith has always been about bright colours."

Art installations in boutiques

In the last twenty years or so, fashion labels have been differentiating themselves and offering consumers not just the purchase of a product, but the purchase of a "lifestyle," saturating the consumer into the brand from homewares and accessories to eateries and exhibition spaces, as labels host cultural and music events as a way of defining their brand. Architect William Russell's design for the Alexander McQueen store in Los Angeles included a sculpture of a human figure by artist Robert Bryce Muir. Titled "Angels of the Americas," the figure is suspended in a light well above the entrance, his head and shoulders appear outside the store, blurring the division between shop and gallery, product and art object. Similarly, the Burberry flagship store in Milan contains a variety of art pieces and installations, including an overhead film that imitates British weather. In 2003, as a way of attracting media attention, and ultimately consumers, Selfridges on Oxford Street became a venue for a performance art installation by Spencer Tunick. "*Body Craze*" contained five hundred naked people who struck a pose on the department store escalators as Tunick photographed the scene. Returning to Paul Smith, the designer's Los Angeles flagship store on Melrose Avenue in West Hollywood is referred to as a "landmark" because of its bright pink wall, which has become an Instagram phenomenon. "When I knew I was getting a shop in Los Angeles," said Paul Smith, "I realized I had to do something with impact, it's now one of the most Instagrammed buildings in California."[41] So much so, that in 2017 Paul Smith collaborated with Instagram and painted a rainbow mural (the brand's signature logo) over the pink wall to celebrate Lesbian, Gay, Bisexual, Transexual, and Queer (LGBTQ) Pride Month (June 5–11). The temporary rainbow wall (before returning to pink) encourages Instagrammers to join the movement by leaving supportive comments on posts (Figure 8). The wall is not intended to draw consumers into the store, but acts as a well-executed exercise in retail branding and social commerce. The wall enhances the Paul Smith label, expands the target audience, and offers Paul Smith consumers the chance to connect with others who share their taste. The store's façade doubles as an installation and as public art, whilst the interior of the store often hosts book-signing events and exhibitions. As part of the Tour de France celebrations, the Paul Smith boutique on rue du Fossé in Luxembourg City hosted an installation by artist James Saffron that drew its theme from cycling. The installation comprised of twelve canvases of Tour de France cycling legends; a set of stencils displaying the twenty municipalities that cyclists passed through on the Luxembourg leg of the race on July, 3 and 4 (2017) and street art in various locations. This was not the first time that Paul Smith and James Saffron had collaborated on an installation to celebrate the Tour de France. As part of Paul Smith's collaboration with Condor Cycles,

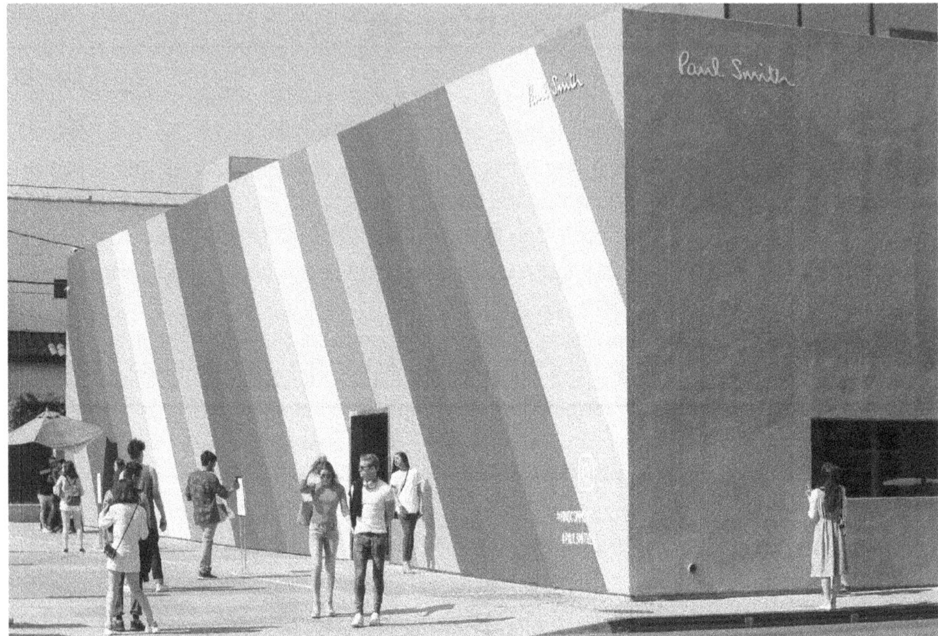

Figure 8 Paul Smith store in stripes, on a sunny day on Melrose Boulevard, June 1, 2017, in Los Angeles, California.

which included garments, bikes, and cycling accessories, Saffron held an exhibition containing a series of artworks that were displayed in the Artwall area of the Globe store at Terminal 5 in Heathrow Airport. "Retailment," the fusion of retail and entertainment such as art exhibitions, book launches, or musical concerts, has become an effective means for luxury fashion labels to generate positive publicity by linking their brand with cultural and intellectual pursuits.

As we have noted in *Fashion and Art* (2012) and *Critical Fashion Practice from Westwood to Van Beirendonck* (2017), several luxury fashion brands have been involved in art sponsorships. Louis Vuitton launched "L'Espace Louis Vuitton" (designed by Frank Gehry), an art exhibition center and book shop within the Paris flagship store on the Avenue des Champs Elysées. As a means of artistic and cultural expression, the center displayed works by contemporary artists such as Vanessa Beecroft (January–March 2006) and Yang Fudong (October 2017–March 2018). There are many other initiatives that support artists, such as the "Furla per l'Arte," a collaboration between the Furla fashion brand and the Italian foundation for art and culture. And then, of course, there is the Prada Fondazioni housed in an old distillery in Milan (designed by Rem Koolhaas), which acts as a contemporary art museum and contains gallery space and a theater for film screenings and live performances and lectures. Bulgari, Rolex, Cartier, and Ermenegildo Zegna are all involved in several art initiatives as a form of retail extension. Such initiatives have not been limited to art, film, literature, and music; fashion brands are now providing the complete shopping and lifestyle experience by offering restaurants, bars, and cafés for the consumer to relax, refuel, and socialize. Food has also been at the center of runway installations, which is not surprising given that food and fashion both choose the body as a site of display and resistance. Noteworthy is the Chanel Fall/Winter 2014/2015 ready-to-wear open-ended runway show that transformed the Grand Palais in Paris into a purpose-built supermarket with specially made Chanel-stamped products (Figure 9). Models paraded down the aisles posing as customers pushing shopping trollies and grabbing products off the shelves. Other models carried shopping baskets with the iconic Chanel handbag chains and talked amongst themselves in the grocery

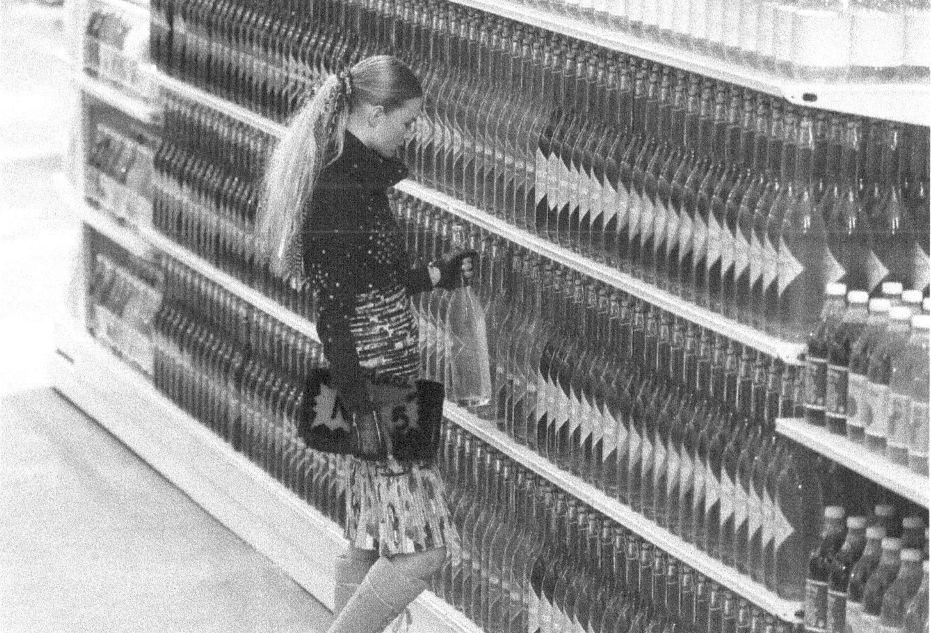

Figure 9 A model walks the runway at the Chanel Fall/Winter 2014/2015 fashion show during Paris Fashion Week on March 4, 2014, in Paris, France.

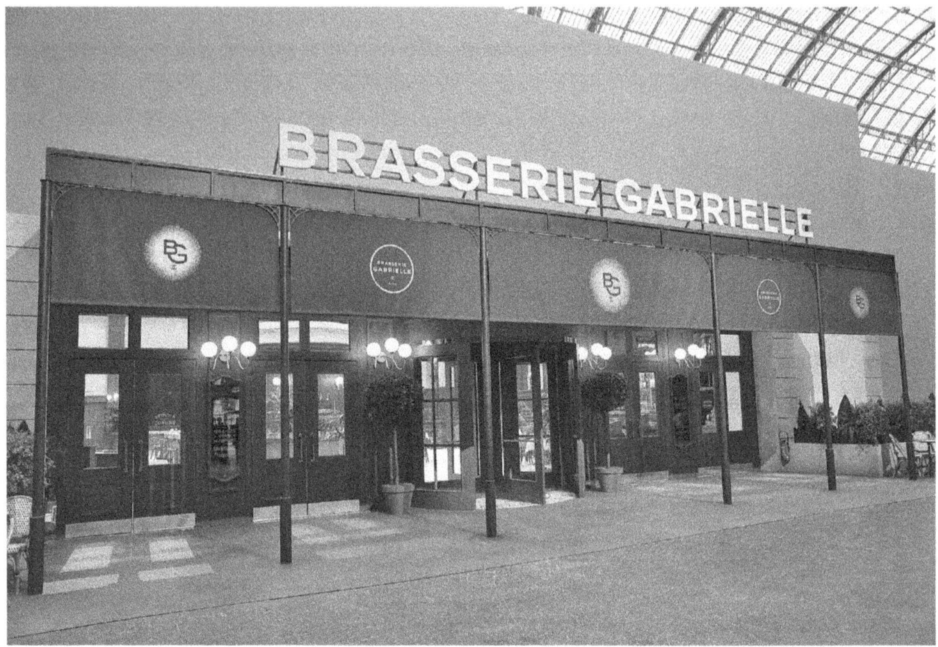

Figure 10 The exterior of Brasserie Gabrielle, Chanel womenswear Fall/Winter 2015/2016, Paris Fashion Week.

aisles. The produce and products all contained the brand's logo in a nod toward consumerism and luxury. "For me the supermarket is the pop art of today," said Karl Lagerfeld, Chanel's creative director.[42]

Keeping in line with the concept of fashion and food, Lagerfeld transformed the Grand Palais into a brasserie-themed runway, the Brasserie Gabrielle to be precise, for Chanel's Fall/Winter 2015/2016 collection (Figure 10). The open-ended installation contained a 360-degree wooden bar, mosaic-tiled floors, and red leather booths. Celebrity Kendall Jenner and model Cara Delevingne sat at the bar as waiters poured drinks on a bar-top covered with baskets of chocolate-filled croissants. Leather-covered booths littered the runway and the front-row-facing tables were covered with white linen (Figure 11). Several bars had been erected throughout the space that served espresso coffee, Champagne, orange juice, and food. As models walked along the restaurant-themed runway, waiters glided amongst the crowd taking orders. The brasserie installation paid homage to French café society.

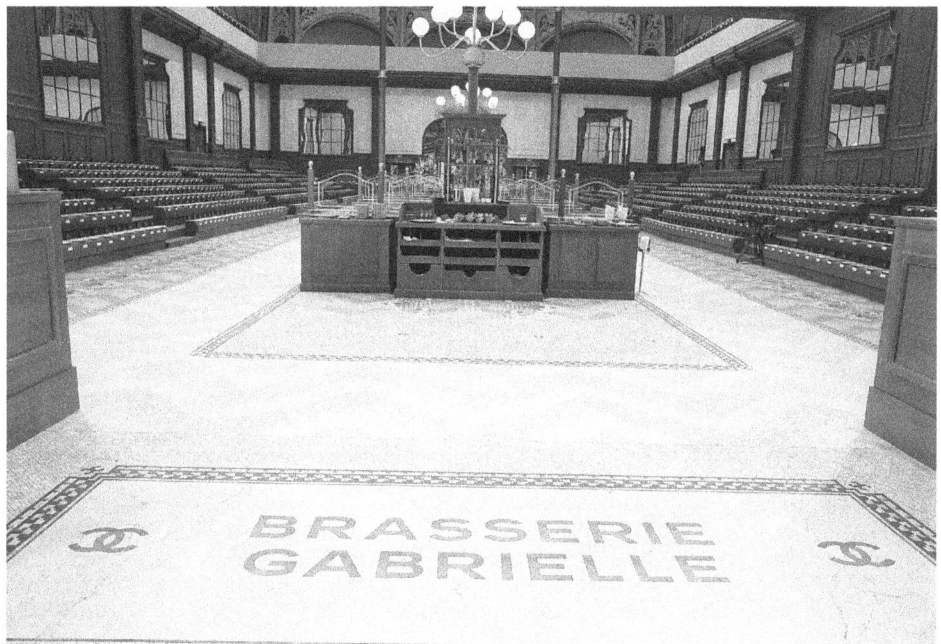

Figure 11 The interior of Brasserie Gabrielle runway installation at the Grand Palais, Chanel womenswear Fall/Winter 2015/2016, Paris Fashion Week.

Gastro-fashion from haute couture to haute cuisine

Maxim's, the world-famous Parisian restaurant on rue Royale, which was established in 1893 and purchased by Pierre Cardin in 1983, contains a private museum and gallery space. Redesigned for the Paris Exposition in 1899, the interior still has the original stained-glass ceiling and Pre-Raphaelite murals of scantily dressed nymphs that are associated with the *Belle Époque* period (Figure 12). The gallery and museum space is comprised of over three levels of Art Nouveau furniture, objects, and artworks in an installation that recreates a courtesan's apartment and intimate boudoir. When Maxim's was opened in 1893, it quickly acquired a reputation as a temple of haute cuisine and a hangout for the super-chic and the rich and famous. The future King Edward VII of England drank Champagne from a dancer's slipper while reclining on a plush red

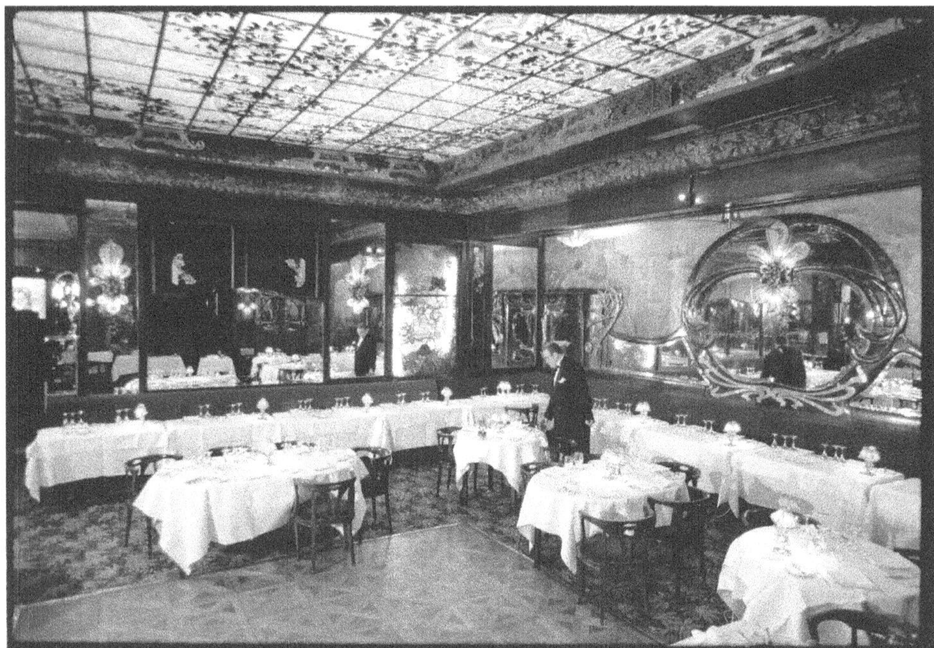

Figure 12 Interior at Maxim's restaurant, Paris.

velvet-covered banquette. Scandalous lovers like shipping magnate Aristotle Onassis and opera singer Maria Callas, or the former Edward VIII and Wallis Simpson, often shared a table.[43] (It is also noteworthy that the restaurant boasts its own label of Champagne.) Maxim's' "racy" reputation was soon memorialized in Franz Lehár's kitsch operetta *The Merry Widow*, as "the place to take ladies but never one's wife,"[44] and in Georges Feydeau's comedy *The Lady from Maxim's*. Declared an historic and cultural monument by the French government, Maxim's has become a trope of the glamour and style that is associated with all things French and fashionable. "Fame is the first essential of licensing [and is] predicated on the transfer of cachet."[45] Considered to be one of the first forays into fashion retail extension and licensing[46] (along with Christian Dior, Givenchy, and Yves Saint Laurent), Cardin's intention was to associate the brand with all the glamour (and scandal) and luxury evoked by the name "Maxim's."

Much has been written about food and its ability to convey meaning, as a system of communication that marks eating practices (Roland Barthes, 1961), food preparation as language (Claude Lévi-Strauss, 1964), and as a way of differentiating class between the taste of luxury and the taste of distinction (Pierre Bourdieu, 1979). In his important book on *Distinction: A Social Critique on the Judgement of Taste* (1979), Bourdieu conducts a critique of taste via the eating habits and spending practices of the French bourgeoisie as a way of asserting distinction. By dividing consumption into a structure that contains three items—food, culture, and presentation (plus clothing and accessories)—Bourdieu analyzes the spending, preparation, and presentation of food as a means of determining difference (including gender). Simply put, the working-class palette (of manual and industrial workers) is defined by spending on large amounts of food; the taste of the bourgeoisie is rich (in cost and calories) with a preference for "heavy, fat and coarse foods" (game, foie gras); as opposed to the "light, defined and delicate tastes" of the professional class (teachers and executives). He writes that the disappearance of monetary restraints is accompanied by an increase in social censorship that forbids "coarseness and fatness" in favor of "slimness and distinction." The "taste for rare, aristocratic foods points to a traditional cuisine rich in expensive and rare products (fresh vegetables, meats)." The teachers, who are richer in cultural rather than economic capital, tend to favor "exotic foods" (Italian, Chinese, etc.) and culinary popularism—what Bourdieu calls "peasant dishes." Teachers, writes Bourdieu,

> are opposed to the new rich [nouveau riche] with their rich food, the buyers and sellers of *grosse bouffe*, the "fat cats", gross in body and mind, who have the economic means to flaunt, with an arrogance perceived as "vulgar", a lifestyle which remains very close to that of the working classes as regards economic and cultural consumption.[47]

What emerges in Bourdieu's social analysis of the French bourgeoisie is that snobbery runs rampant and that the aesthetic choices people of each class make are different from and in opposition to those choices made by other classes. In other words, the social world functions as a system of power relations and as a symbolic system whereby distinctions of taste become the basis for social judgment. Norbert Elias believed that the cultural practices of the elites "percolated" down to the rest of the classes, so that the lower classes emulated the elites, causing the latter to reinvent themselves in order to remain distinctive and superior.[48] Elias' argument stands very close to Thorstein Veblen's study of the leisured class (*The Theory of the Leisure Class: An Economic Study of Institutions*, 1899), which is considered a foundational text in the study of fashion. In short, Veblen's study of conspicuous consumption shows that fashion flows vertically from the upper social classes to the lower classes, each class being influenced by the class above. As lower social groups seek to establish a higher status by adopting and "imitating" the fashions of the higher social groups, the higher social groups adopt new fashions to differentiate themselves and give an indication of their wealth. Bourdieu's, Elias', and Veblen's research is useful in understanding the connection between fashion and food as an indicator of wealth and taste. Take, after all, the fashion for *nouvelle cuisine* in which taste, design, flair, and appearance preside over quantity. The conspicuous consumption here is the display of how little one needs to consume—form over substance.

The trend towards the development of cafés, bars, and restaurants by luxury brands is yet another form of "retailment" as fashion labels create branded environments that people literally consume and digest. Combining art installation with food, a vast majority of luxury fashion labels are now offering what we have called "gastrofashion" as part of the shopping experience. The Dolce and Gabbana boutique on Corzo Venezia in Milan contains the Martini Bar and Bistrôt which offers consumers an experiential environment of Milan in the 1950s. The bar and Bistrôt is a collaboration between Dolce and Gabbana and the Martini aperitif made famous by the playboy spy James Bond 007 and Federico Fellini's classic *La Dolce Vita* (The Sweet Life, 1960), a film that follows gossip columnist Marcello Rubini over the span of a week as he journeys through "the sweet life" in Rome searching for love and happiness. The interior of the gastro space, with the neon Martini signage and logo suspended above the bar and the black glossy surfaces, is intended to conjure an association with the good times (or boom times) of Italy in the 1950s, a time of massive economic growth and prosperity, and a period of momentous change in Italian design and culture. The automobile industry, Fiat, Vespa, Alpha Romeo, and Pirelli, coupled with the Italian film industry and smaller craft and design-based companies, placed Italy on the international map. Bar Martini doubled as the site for D&G's invitation-only "Secret Show" as part of Spring/Summer 2017 Milan Fashion Week, bringing fashion and food together.

As part of their retailment strategy, Prada acquired the historic Italian pastry shop Pasticeria Marchessi (1824) and opened a second location in Milan. Its chartreuse- and pastel-colored upholstery is teamed up with Prada's Fall 2015 collection. Coincidence? We think not. At the back of the store is an intimate dining area where customers can linger. And then there is Gucci's Osteria, a fifty-seat, green-walled restaurant in the Gucci Garden inside the Palazzo della Mercanzia, which contains the Gucci Galleria Museum, whose rooms are curated by fashion critic Maria Luisa Frisa (Figure 13). The Museum is divided into a series of curated rooms that spans across two levels. Inside the "Guccification" space hangs the graffiti-style Double G logo by artist Trouble Andrews, who goes by the moniker "Gucci Ghost." Andrews collaborated with creative director Alessandro Michele on the Fall/Winter 2016 collection. "Paraphernalia" contains signature codes and symbols that define the brand's identity, and "Cosmorama" displays Gucci objects and accessories. On the upper level of the Museum is the Cinema de Camera that features a preview of *Zeus Machine/Phoenix*, a short film by Zapruder filmmakers' group and the De Rerum Natura, a curated room in the style of a natural history museum. "Ephemera" contains objects, videos, and memorabilia that trace the history of the Gucci brand.

Figure 13 A general view of the atmosphere at the Gucci Museum opened on September 26, 2011 in Florence, Italy.

The installation of a dedicated food space in a shopping environment is not anything new, as department stores and shopping malls have been serving food to consumers since the early twentieth century. What has changed is the type of consumer that luxury fashion brands are hoping to attract, the millennial generation, people in their early twenties and mid-thirties, known as the "food generation," or simply "foodies." Much like pop-up shops whose purpose is to introduce a brand to a new, younger consumer and create a loyal following, fashion brands are providing a social environment where millennials can socialize with friends as well as purchase products. Millennials have grown up on a spate of television cooking programs and food stars of the 1980s and 1990s, such as Jamie Oliver, Nigella Lawson, and Gordon Ramsay. They buy gluten-free artisan bread, drink craft beer, and eat *nudja*, the pork salami that comes in a jar. They are part of the slow food movement and believe in the sustainable farming practices of paddock to plate and nose to tail. In sum, they live at home, spend more money on food than any other previous generation,[49] and their key interests revolve around fashion and friends. "Just as people have always sought to express who they are through the clothes they wear and possessions they own, Gen Z and millennials will further explore and express their identity

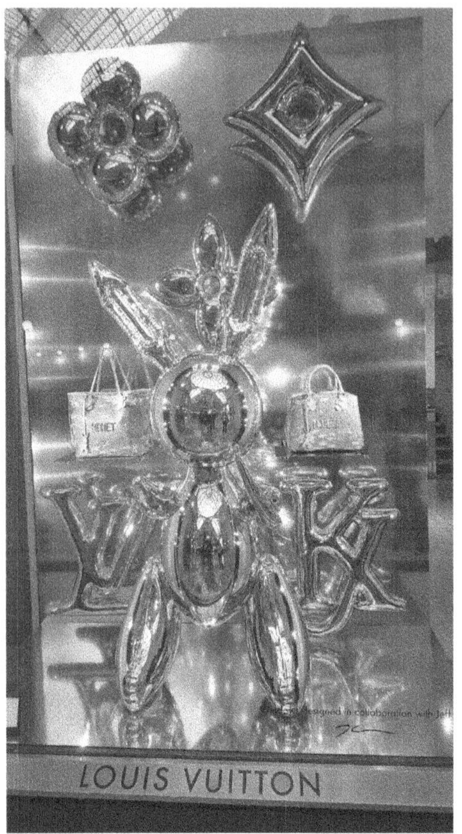
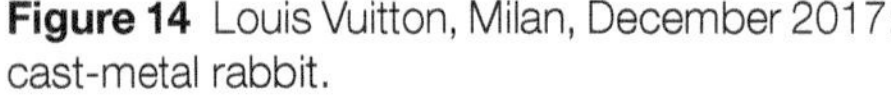
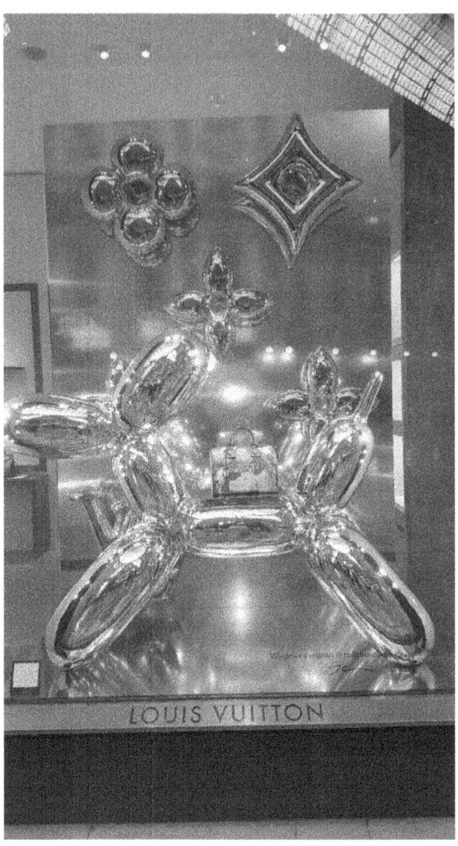

Figure 14 Louis Vuitton, Milan, December 2017: cast-metal rabbit.

Figure 15 Louis Vuitton, Milan, December 2017: balloon dog.

through the foods they eat [and the food they wear]," said Wanda Pogue, chief strategist for advertising firm Saatchi & Saatchi. "Food has become just another platform for self-expression for both consumers and companies—a way to express creativity and even their sense of design."[50]

In 2017, Vuitton enlisted Jeff Koons to design a series of window displays for their stores worldwide, from Nice to Paris to Milan and New York. Koons responded with his by then signature objects that he had rolled out in numerous exhibitions, including one at the Versailles Palace: the lustrous cast-metal rabbit dating from early in his career, to the enlarged metallic balloon dog which has enjoyed innumerable iterations (Figures 14 and 15). These stood against shimmering grounds together with similar "Koonsified" versions of the Vuitton brand pattern. It was a curious, if predictable, "collaboration," to use a fashionable and often misused term. Curious because of the synergy, or rather, the reciprocity of brand-sign. Who was endorsing who? When fashion enlists art to its ends, fashion always comes out the better, because of the hierarchy it seeks to overturn. Here, there were no goods, no people, just stand-ins for value. The surfeit of shine, gloss, and reflection left no room for doubt, as it seldom does with Koons (or Vuitton). All one was presented with was value+value+value *ad infinitum* in a vertiginous display to the point of nausea. This was contemporary art and fashion taken to an end point. Who needs reality when all you need is display?

3
BODY-IN-SPACE AND THE *GESAMTKUNSTWERK*

A recurring theme throughout this book is the question as to the locus of fashion: fashion, where is it? The difficulty in situating the fashion experience is exacerbated by the expectation of fashion's fleetingness. By now it is a platitude to state that fashion does not simply reside in the garment. It exists first as a representation, and as association, finding itself within time in narrative action. As Benjamin formulated it, greater time can be strikingly perceived in the fragmentary and the transient as opposed to an abstract whole. Fashion's genesis in modernity has always occurred together with developments in technology. With fashion as an ideological and economic system developed out of the eighteenth-century parallel with popular print media, including the early newspaper. Fashion as haute couture arose at roughly the same time as the introduction of photography, and by early in the next century, it made voracious use of film. Thus, fashion's seemingly natural evolution was toward building an environment for itself that either improved upon the real world, or presented alternative worlds. Since fashion in theory and in its physical consumption is a mixture of a multitude of elements and factors, its culmination at the end of the twentieth century into multimedia spectacles can be seen as an inevitable outcome to what is immanent to the fashion system. Fashion installations have become examples of what Richard Wagner called the *Gesamtkunstwerk*, or "total work of art," a harmonized combination of all the arts. Typically, these exist today as live performances, such as the catwalk, as an art/fashion installation, as a film, or as fashion film as it is now widely known. We have divided contemporary fashion installation into three simple categories: open-ended, sealed, or closed and still. The former applies to a catwalk show in which the audience is incorporated, even as an audience, to some degree, the latter is used for *still* fashion installations, such as those on display in a museum or art gallery context and for films and for fashion shows in which the action is more or less discrete.

The *Gesamtkunstwerk*

The notion of the *Gesamtkunstwerk* has enjoyed some revival in the last few decades, in no small part through the introduction of video art into artistic mainstream practice, and with the revival of performance art since the early years of the millennium, which also made use of video as medium for its dissemination beyond the single event. In the early years of the twenty-first century, arguably the most active buzz-word in art and related theories was "new media," what turned out to be an indefinite umbrella term for media using or processed by a digital interface. At the time, video and video art were categorized under the new media rubric, and the *Gesamtkunstwerk* enjoyed greater circulation amongst artists and theorists, although it had previously been used as a way of understanding cinema. Today, the overall prevalence of the moving image for anyone with access to a digital device makes it a form that is axiomatic, and melded smoothly into everyone's life—from Facetime to YouTube to Snapchat—and integral to contemporary interpersonal relations.

However, the *Gesamtkunstwerk* may be allowed to have yet another renaissance when thinking about the contemporary catwalk as it evolved in the same years as the rise of digital media in art, design, and everyday life. For while it is commonplace to use the image in catwalk displays, when they are live, they are a component to a spectacle that is of a piece with the most sophisticated stage design and art direction. The contemporary catwalk reveals an active and lively cross-pollination between theater and opera design, as well as both arthouse and commercial film art direction. The object of fashion, assumed simplistically to be the garment "itself," becomes swallowed into what Benjamin called "phantasmagoria," a saturation of specular stimuli, so that the object of fashion is revealed to be the event itself. When not live, in fashion film, the body and garment become the locus, or the ciphers, for truncated narratives, through to digital manipulations that sever any relations to the so-called "real," outside world.

Originally coined in 1827 by the philosopher and theologian Karl F. E. Trahndorff in his study of aesthetics,[1] *Gesamtkunstwerk* became used more widely as a result of two essays by Richard Wagner, penned in 1849 and later developed in 1852.[2] Although it remains unclear whether Wagner knew of Trahndorff's coinage, he became an advocate of the term to describe what he argued was his unique and groundbreaking contribution to opera, drama, and art as a whole. Other thinkers in the German Romantic tradition, with which Trahndorff identified, had already begun discussing the prospects of a fusion of the arts, with the exemplar regularly gravitating to opera. Around this era, the accepted classic text of the separation of the arts, and an argument that different arts convey different emotions and ideas, was the meditation over the Hellenic sculpture *Lakoön and his Sons* by Gotthold Ephraim Lessing from 1766. But the Romantics tired of what they deemed aesthetic stringency and observed the way artistic disciplines were challenging their formal parameters. In revising Lessing's legacy, in 1854 Gustav Freytag argued that there were changes afoot not only in the novel, "but almost all the other arts, in painting as in music" in which "there is an evident striving to overstep boundaries." True to a Romantic cadence, this overstepping was tantamount to shifting from the barriers of mortality to the eternal.[3] Wagner's own conception harkened back to the idea of the ancient Greeks as a climax in human development. But once the "Athenian Polis" fell, the arts diverge to become fractured, separated, and thereby significantly weakened. The arts left on their own had limited potential for development of expression. As Wagner proclaimed, "Today each of the single arts can no longer offer us anything new."[4]

Emboldened by the revolutions that occurred across Europe in 1848, Wagner boldly asserted that a corollary existed between a fusion of the arts and social cohesion.[5] By comparison to how they had once existed, the discrete arts had been divested of their original potential, one that he saw himself restoring in his operas, which some would later call "music dramas." His ideas found their most influential embodiment in *The Ring of the Nibelung*, or *Ring Cycle* (1848–1874), *Tristan and Isolde* (1857–1859), and *Parsifal* (1877–1882). These presented, to Wagner's mind and those of his followers, the apotheosis of art in its cohesion of music, drama, poetry, dance, painting, and sculpture (the latter two in the stage designs and in the visual tableaux). The extent of this achievement, and how it could be measured, is highly contestable; nonetheless, Wagner's ideas and work would continue to resonate in the nineteenth and early twentieth centuries, influencing not only composers, but writers, dramatists, and architects. Many of the experiments that took place at the Bauhaus, for instance, acknowledged his influence.

In the early days of film and its growth into a major industry, Wagner's ideas found new appeal. From the very beginning of the twentieth century, theorists and film-makers alighted onto the concept of the *Gesamtkunstwerk*, especially in regard to the notion of a synthesis, "one which," as Carolyn Birdsall explains, "was initially based on the relationship of (visual) cinematic techniques and narrative."[6] But such analogies gained in vigor with the introduction of sound to cinema in the 1920s. And the notion of specular totalities were also enthusiastically taken up in theory and practice by National Socialism for their films and rallies, not only for advancing an aggressive and persuasive displays for their own might, but also because of Wagner's own rabid anti-Semitism. As Birdsall continues, "Synchronized sound film, too, in unifying sound and image, was appropriated after 1933 as a prime example of the Wagnerian synaesthesic model for German nationalism."[7] Cinemas had designated spaces not only for experience of the commonality of the German *Volk*, but also as means of driving home the speed and efficiency of technological advances.[8] Newsreels, dubbed with voices and heroic music, gained in grandiosity as preparations for the war effort gained in momentum. Yet it is noteworthy that such aesthetic effusiveness did not lend itself to newsreels that recorded mounting German defeats from 1942 onward.[9] It is also this historically and ethically compromised set of coordinates, between Wagner's anti-Semitic nationalism, Nazism, and the forceful, massed fusion of the arts, that subsequently brought the concept of the *Gesamtkunstwerk* into disrepute.

Yet the experimental arts of the 1960s and 1970s caused a resurgence of the idea, due to the way in which normative boundaries were broken, which introduced degrees of theatricality. As Julia Cloot remarks, artistic tendencies such as Fluxus, Happenings, *Aktionismus*, performance have to be seen against developments in dance, theater, and music. That is, the work of conceptual, installation, and performance artists has to be evaluated against the work of someone like John Cage and composers such as Karlheinz Stockhausen.[10] In many respects, Cloot contends, Wagner's *Gesamtkunstwerk* becomes realized with the "media arts" of the twenty-first century, with their combinations of music, space, and sound, while unencumbered by Wagner's high-minded mythological and nationalistic baggage.[11]

Other words that have been used contemporaneously with the rise of digital technologies in the arts include "intermedia," "intermediality," "transmedia," and the better-known "multimedia," which is a term whose use is not limited to art. The earlier debates of the beginning of the nineteenth century still pertain when evaluating such approaches to art (and design); namely, whether "more is more," and what purpose the fusion of the arts, an additive as opposed to reductive approach, serves other than to create something bigger than life. Magnitude was certainly an aim of Wagner, and evaluated within the realms of his own aesthetic and style (if one is able to leave aside his nationalism and anti-Semitism), it yields its satisfactions, but the question that remains is whether aesthetic magnitude need be *de rigueur*, and it is one that can definitely be applied to the contemporary world of fashion.

One answer to this comes in the figure of Andy Warhol. Warhol, who never used or cared for the term, was, however, in no uncertain terms a major exponent of the *Gesamtkunstwerk*, especially when taking into account his studio, the Factory, which can be considered a mobile and multifaceted work of art. As Annette Michelson asserts,

> it was Warhol's strength to have revised the notion of the *Gesamtkunstwerk*, displacing it, redefining it as a site of production, and recasting it in the mode of the carnival, thereby generating for our time the most trenchant articulation of relation between cultures, high and low. In the picture of carnival as a system of representation, we can recognize the old Factory, that hall of mirrors whose virtual space generated improbable encounters and alliances, eliciting extravagant acts, gestures, "numbers", that composed the serial parody of Hollywood production that overtakes the Warholian filmography of 1960–68.[12]

Written in 1991, Michelson's observations now have prophetic relevance to fashion installation, especially with the way it confounds high and low culture through carnival. Indeed, it is also evident that there is a genre of fashion film (several by Lagerfeld, for example) that engage in a parody of Hollywood, through a similar strategy used by Warhol, namely camp. And as in fashion's installation and its attendant *Gesamtkunstwerke*, with Warhol there is no recourse or suggestion of a "real" outside world, but rather he presents an unapologetic and ecstatic new creation, where decadence and excess are devices within the system, not symptoms of a condition.

Open-ended installations

Alexander McQueen

The debt that mainstream and high culture owe to Alexander McQueen has been widely acknowledged, as his influence has extended well beyond the fashion industry to film, fashion film, and music video. His influence in both traditional and nascent moving image genres is due in no small part to the encompassing—and to use the word made popular in the 1990s to characterize video installation, "immersive"—nature of his catwalk shows. Beginning in the early 1990s, since his graduation collection in 1992, by the mid-1990s these became ever more complex productions that drew from pre-sound cinema, film noir and contemporary horror film, art history (especially Surrealism), musicals and vaudeville, as well as style trends in music such as Glam and the New Romantics. The audience became part of an event in which the lines between materiality (of the actual garment to life itself) and fantasy all but collapsed. McQueen did not take long to become a designer with a distinctive look, and one of the most compelling aspects of his approach to fashion is that it was impossible to discern whether the shows were a vehicle for the garments or the garments for the shows. With some exceptions, which we will also detail in this chapter, McQueen is one of a handful of fashion designers who introduces a new terrain, and a new mentality, to fashion design. Fashion design had always been a bedfellow to cinema, to art, music, and theater; however, with McQueen's catwalk shows they all seem to converge with such imaginative intensity that one gets the impression that the history of the fashion show had been leading up to this. It is as if in retrospect a teleology could be traced from the tendencies of the past and the climax occurred at the end of the millennium.

A distinctive and original aspect of McQueen's approach, especially for the mid-1990s, was to see his collections as a show. As Janet Fischgrund, McQueen's promotional manager from 1997, remarks, "The ideas were what were important to him, the clothes were his canvas in a way."[13] Beginning with the operative framework of a story, a concept, a provocation of some sort, McQueen approached his collections in a manner that a contemporary artist would approach a show, in which the title served as the umbrella for theme, or connected themes, which the respective works would exemplify. It is this cogency of the work as a corpus that is so important to installation, for the idea of a title under which all the works co-exist also implies that the viewer is somehow subsumed into the embrace of the work. While each art object, or garment, may have had effectiveness on their own, in the better interests of the "*Gesamt,*" their better impetus was as a collective.

This need to propel fashion into imaginary spaces came very early for McQueen, even in his early years working for Givenchy. Even then, in these relatively early stages of his career, states Susannah Frankel,

> his shows, increasingly, had more in common with art installations than anything more obviously consumer-driven by nature. McQueen sent his models out onto a raised Plexiglass catwalk filled with ink-stained water and showered with golden rain (*Untitled* spring/summer 1998). *Joan* (autumn/winter 1998–99) featured a lava runway exploding into flames. *The Overlook* (autumn/winter 1999–2000) was dominated by a larger-than-life snowstorm inside which models appeared in ice skates, opulent jacquards, and furs.[14]

Similarly, Andrew Bolton avers that McQueen shows suggested "installation and performance art."[15] For although McQueen was a talented tailor, he would never let technicalities get in the way of his broader vision, which was a reflection of his emotional as well as political state of mind. He saw his role as more than simply a designer, each collection enshrined some form of social commentary: "I'm making points about my time, about the times we live in. My work is a social document of the world today."[16] It is an attitude that, while far from unique, would accelerate the pull toward the recognition that fashion could be a powerful vector of social critique. After all, fashion and dress are never too distant in the envisioning of self in relation to the collective.

McQueen's first explicit homage to film came with his Spring/Summer collection, "The Hunger," which, with its dark and ghastly overtones, made clear reference to the 1983 cult horror film *The Hunger*, directed by Tony Scott. Starring David Bowie, Catherine Deneuve, and Susan Sarandon, the film, which quickly became a neo-goth cult classic, tells of two vampires, Miriam (Deneuve) and John (Bowie). An unusual twist in the vampire genre is that the turned vampire, John, begins to age after two hundred years, remaining alive but in an eternal state of decrepitude. We later learn that all of Miriam's former lovers remain preserved in vaults, living out eternity in wizened oblivion. For McQueen, whose sensibility was always tipped toward death, this was an opportunity to continue his experiments with the macabre, with printed veins on fabrics, and sleeves that suggested straightjackets. In one of the looks, worms escaped from out of a plastic bodice-bustier. The detail of the story of the aged undead also provides a cogent narrative for the passages of fashion, where old lines are re-worn and live on, but imbued with an irretrievable quality of the past, an irretrievability that is only emphasized each time such a garment is worn.

The ensuing collection was a decisive step for McQueen into the fashion *Gesamtkunstwerk*, and a continuation with the theme of death. For the 1996/1997 Fall/Winter collection, "Dante," the catwalk was held unconventionally in a church. Models wearing masks bearing a cruciform strutted or stalked the aisles. Slashed bleached denim appeared alongside black lace. At the beginning, the blasted music of the organ was terminated by the sound of gunfire. Those who sat in the front row, reserved for the elite fashion press, had to share it with a skeleton, sitting gingerly on the pew. It is now hard to imagine how the audience reacted, although it was all orchestrated to elicit a dazed and uneasy response—cast into a Dantean hell. A recurring motif with McQueen is that beauty must be apprehended together with what it excludes or represses, which is ugliness and death. And in contemplating beauty we are soon gripped by the terror of its transience.

The 1997 Spring/Summer collection entitled "La Poupée" was in direct reference to the work and the book published by the German Surrealist artist Hans Bellmer. It is generally agreed that the impetus for the disturbing imagery in the limited edition book *Die Puppe* (1934) owes itself to the triumph of Hitler and the National Socialists and their rise to power in 1933.[17] Although he was also a highly accomplished draftsman, Bellmer is best known for his monstrously de-articulated doll forms, which began as *papier mâché* sculptures that were then photographed in interiors and in forests. These are dolls that are articulated with ball joints which are then pulled apart and re-assembled in perverse ways that connote brutality: heads and appendages are not in the right places, sometimes legs in one direction are rhymed with legs in the opposite direction. And the dolls are arranged in a splayed and tortured manner. While doubtlessly vulnerable to accusations of misogyny, for Bellmer these adolescent "girls" brought into a state of jarring deformity were the symbols of the most supreme violation, and for that they presaged the atrocities that were to occur during the next decade and later. Given that his 1995/1996 Fall/Winter collection was called "Highland Rape," McQueen's attraction to Bellmer's project seems perfectly in order, as they introduce us to a scabrous and adulterated world that is bereft of hope and whose beauty is only a memory.

Translating this into the fashion, McQueen emphasized the body as an aggregate of discrete parts, which in the artificial state could be removed and returned. McQueen was seldom, if ever, inclined to treat the body as some natural, autonomous core on which garments were hung. Rather, he played with the silhouette, widening hips and shoulders, or created garments to which the body had to conform. To stylize and hamper natural movement, the catwalk, measuring around 30 meters, was covered in water. One of the more controversial transformations was as a result of a piece of "contortion" jewelry, comprised of two metal bars, one spanning the elbows, the other the knees, deployed to make the model's (Debra Shaw) movements jerky, in the manner of a mechanized puppet.[18] For McQueen, the body is a surface in which the line between what is real and what is prosthesis is more or less disavowed, abandoned.

McQueen would reprise the theme of the interface of body and mechanics, and the aesthetics of prosthetics, in the runway show "No. 13" (Spring/Summer 2000), a collection that lives on today simply because its imagery is so vividly reproducible. The models were placed on turntables like music-box ballerinas. Skirts were made of balsa wood and the dresses were heavily embroidered with crystals. A memorable and celebrated part of the show was the appearance at the opening of the Paralympian athlete Aimee Mullins — whose lower legs had been amputated when she was one year old as a result of missing fibula bones (fibular hemimelia) — appearing in tight leather bodice over a light, ruffled lace skirt, and wearing two sculpted prosthetic legs.[19] Instead of her sprinting legs, for which she was best known, these were of carved stained wood in the shape of boots, and were decorated with bas-relief Art Nouveau-like floral tendrils. The heel was tapered and splayed like the boots of the *fin de siècle* nineteenth century. For the climax of the show, the model Shalom Harlow wore a large splayed white dress secured above the bust with a leather belt. This was then sprayed in black and yellow by two machines on either side of her whose regular function was to paint cars.

Arguably McQueen's most famous catwalk production, "Voss" (later nicknamed the "Asylum Collection," Spring/Summer 2001), was also the most costly, at seventy thousand pounds. (The title itself is another indication of the sheer oddity of the show and the matching collection: Voss is a region in south-west Norway, a common German surname, and the title of a novel by the Australian Nobel Prize-winner Patrick White, yet McQueen's collection appears to relate to none of these.) Taking a week to construct, the centerpiece was a massive glass box, which stood in for the catwalk or stage. After all the invitees had found their seats, the box was left to mirror the audience for an unprecedented amount of time, to general discomfort and mild consternation. (This first sequence is now widely seen as a commentary on the vanity and narcissism of the fashion world.) This first phase of the show, which in many ways conjoins our constructed topology of "open" versus "closed" environments for presenting collections, is widely read as a commentary of the fashion world itself, and its overweening vanity. In this case, the designer made the audience itself the space of its own desire. Once the audience was suitably unnerved, the box lit up, revealing the models that watched their own movements through the two-way mirror. One

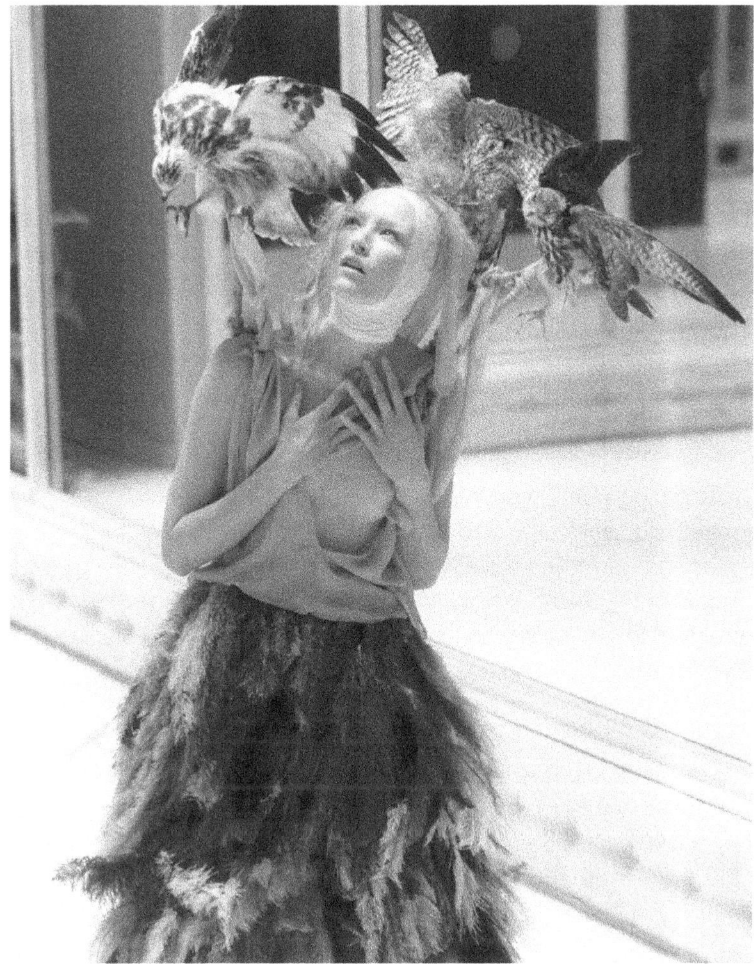

Figure 16 A model presents a creation by Alexander McQueen for the Spring/Summer collection at London Fashion Week, September 26, 2000.

model had her shoulders bedecked by a small menagerie of taxidermied birds of prey (kites and falcons) (Figure 16). As to McQueen's ongoing interest in animals in his garments and catwalk shows, Stephen Seely remarks that:

McQueen's work creates … zones of proximity through the incorporation of animal and other natural features into his garments. According to Deleuze and Guattari, becoming always involves a "third term", a "something else" that opens the individual up to the normally imperceptible process of becoming and generates the proximity between two entities required for mutual becoming.[20]

In other words, the use of animals urges new possibilities by pointing to spaces that exist beyond the "normal," "natural" body, which includes the conventional body–garment relation. What is generated is a rhetorically performative space.

If the beginning had not been unsettling, the most enigmatic part of all was the glass box within the glass box, containing a plus-size model on a chaise longue wearing a saturnine mask, sucking from a thick catheter, calling to mind a participant in a Roman orgy, yet transformed into something belonging to some arcane sado-masochistic Saturnalia. The glass walls of this box then fell, the glass shattering on the floor all around. The reclining model was, in the words of Evans:

> The fetish writer Michelle Olley reclining on a lace-covered sofa made from huge cow horns. Based on Joel-Peter Witkin's photograph "Sanitarium" of a twenty-stone middle-aged woman, connected via a breathing tube to a stuffed monkey, Olley's bandaged head was covered in a pig-mask of ghostly grey, a breathing pipe apparently protruding from her mouth, while her body was covered in large, fragile moths. Some were attached to her, others fluttered loose in the box. In the staging of this show, McQueen oscillated between beauty and horror, turning conventional ideas of beauty upside down.[21]

As the *pièce de résistance*, what was also predominant was the absence, in the traditional sense, of clothing, of fashion. The naked figure was a paradoxical combination of hypertrophy and lack. Where was "fashion"? It lay in the air, in the gesture, and the indelible stamp of the image in the minds of those who held the memory. In this regard, McQueen had distilled fashion into its basest elements, being all the intangibles of perception and desire.

The unforgettable bizarreness of "Voss" has tended to overshadow the ensuing collection, "What a Merry-Go-Round" (Fall/Winter 2001/2002), although it was just as original, compelling, and sinister. Just as "Dante" took place in a church, this collection was launched at an actual merry-go-round site in front of a Victorian toy store, but with somber lighting to take advantage of the chilling, uncanny character. The circus rounds were deprived of people and play, amplifying the eerie dimension of the doll. Rendering the air of fête and fun a distant shadow, the make-up artist Val Garland—who has also worked on a number of McQueen collections—painted the models as sad clowns. Together with their violent, conical hairstyles, they became spectral and vampiric. Their impression, to quote Evans, was "mournful and alienated."[22] McQueen had already played with a similar narrative and aesthetic in "The Overlook" (Fall/Winter, 1999/2000), where the audience sat on the fringes of an artificial landscape of ghostly, wintry white. The models skated around small mounds of fake snow and trees, illuminated by cold blue light. Both scenarios pointed directly to the loss of childhood innocence, with "The Overlook" suggesting Narnia's Ice Queen, and "What a Merry-Go-Round" an erstwhile place of childhood play degraded by haunting and sadness. Instead of being figures of envy or bearers of beauty, McQueen has his models as predators and phantoms. With a nod to the "Dante" collection, one model drags a shining brass skeleton behind her. In an act of valediction, another model severs a bunch of balloons and lets them fly away.

Much as "Voss" was a commentary on the fashion world, "What a Merry-Go-Round" portrayed fashion as a madhouse and a circus, a site of haunted relics and quashed dreams. This is also not to forget that fashion shows, with their swarm of journalists and hangers on are often referred to as the "fashion circus." It is a phrase that captures the frenetic, spectacular theatricality of the event, as well as its excess, frivolity, and evanescence. The circus is the home of mannequins and dolls, and like dolls the circus has a duality, its darker side threatening disorientation and loss. In the catwalk show, the models used a pole on which to turn, pole-dancer style, but something lent an air of grotesquerie to those in semi-drag. The somber aggressiveness of the clothes, the movements, the music, and the setting, conveyed a subtle message that the models were there under sufferance, and that the purpose of their presence was to hide some darker secret.

"What a Merry-Go-Round" offers some profound insights into the so-called "space of fashion," especially of high fashion on the international stage. For, on the one hand, the audience may marvel at the confident mastery of the event, its elegance and its daring, bringing home once again that "real life" is just a secondary facsimile of how things are in an imaginary elsewhere. On the other hand, the figures that deliver this sense to us are dolls, insensate ciphers operating to a blueprint or script, condemned to act according to the puppet-master's plan. They act for someone else and for the sake of others. The "space of fashion," then, exists somewhere between these two states, two poles of non-life and the imaginary. Fashion's life, as McQueen's work so urgently and persistently expresses, occurs as a result of, and despite, the impassable ambit of death.

But it was not only McQueen who dabbled in the spectacular and the illusionary to draw the audience into fantastical worlds with his catwalk shows; John Galliano was also staging shows that paralleled McQueen in their elaborate themes. Although Galliano and McQueen were contemporaries, differing aspects of British popular culture influenced their design aesthetic. For Galliano, it was punk and 1980s New Romantic music, with the likes of Adam Ant and the swashbuckling pirate tradition. For McQueen, who arrived a little later to the London fashion scene, it was the photography of Joel-Peter Witkin and Hans Bellmer ("Voss" and "La Poupee") and often alluded to literary works ("Dante" and "The Island of Dr. Moreau") and films, such as Alfred Hitchcock for "The Birds" collection. Having said this, Galliano and McQueen shared many similarities, including a working-class background and time spent in the theater before commencing their careers in fashion design. The theatrical tradition of spectacle, exaggerated performance, and sound and lighting to produce the "total work of art," or *Gesamtkunstwerk*, is evidenced in catwalk productions that contained characters, locations, and recognizable themes. Michael Specter wrote that Galliano "thinks about fashion shows the way Steven Spielberg thinks about movies. He believes in spectacle, complication, suspense."[23] The same can be said about McQueen, who liked to shock and inspire controversy with his themed shows. It can also be said that Galliano and McQueen were historical revisionists who plundered from the annals of history (much like Vivienne Westwood) for the themes that accompanied their catwalk productions. Assemblages of references to assorted eras, places, cultures, and times were cobbled together to produce imaginary places of awe and beauty for Galliano or shock and horror in the case of McQueen. Whether their intentions were to shock, entertain, or simply to sell clothes, the combination of theater, fashion, art, and performance, what Ginger Gregg Duggan calls "cross-media spectacles,"[24] succeeded in creating nothing less than spectacles of excess. Caroline Evans writes that in the 1990s, fashion historicism, the romantic reconfiguring of the past into the present, came mainly from European, in particular British, designers. However, these troubling historical returns "were not the quaint and picturesque version of history usually referred to by fashion, but a darker, more despairing re-run of the past."[25]

Hussein Chalayan

Closely predating McQueen's powerful 2001 shows, for the presentation of his Fall/Winter 2000/2001 collection, Hussein Chalayan pulled what could be called a creative coup. Four models walk into a stark white domestic interior that is redolent of modernist absurdist theatre, the room-stage is all white, containing only four chairs, a round, low coffee-table, and something like a television. The walls are angular as opposed to parallel to the floor, and the chamber is rhomboid. There are two doors, ajar. Behind a white scrim are four figures, the Bulgarka Junior Quartet, singing a song that is like a discordant folk chant. Four models enter the room, they wear simple pale gray dresses, like slips, and their hair is shaped into black Brancusi-esque sculptural shapes. They remove the gray chair covers and invert the fabric, revealing them to be garments, which they proceed to don. Once re-clothed, they line up to face the audience while two men, like stage hands changing the set during the performance typical to formalist post-Brechtian theater, reconfigure the chairs into suitcases, which they position to the left side of each of the models. They stand still like dolls. A fifth model then appears, walks to the coffee-table and removes a small circular disk. She then enters the form and pulls it up for it to become a circular ziggurat-like dress that she fastens to her waist. She then joins the four other models, while the musical quartet close with strained shrieks.[26]

The economy and configuration of this installation-performance are such that one is led to ask whether its meaning is to promote a suite of clothes or whether it is about something else. Certainly, the circumscriptions placed around the number of clothes—five models, one wearing something that few would want to wear—points to this. Unlike the conventional catwalk, Chalayan causes us to think about an approach to clothing, in the sense of the verb, not the noun. He also draws attention to our relationship between our bodies and to objects and the ways in which they can be coeval and co-altered. Even if the garments showed evident artfulness, Chalayan, in the manner of the best conceptual fashion design, offers us an idea. The formalist modernist theater of the mid-twentieth century that is so strong here is brought into collision with another approach in architecture ventured at the same time. Here, architects such as Hannes Meyer, Marcel Breuer, and Le Corbusier employed a modular approach to building and design in which the parts were made to stand equal to the sum, so that each architectural unit, or passage, was like a microcosm of the aggregate structure. Similarly, Chalayan emphasizes reconfiguring, denaturing, refolding, reforming as part of the garment's meaning, or better, its life. The chant is an aesthetic foil to the angularity and structured nature of the performance, a way of bringing it back down to the messiness of life.

John Galliano

Galliano's models often encourage audience participation in his runway shows: for Fall/Winter 1997/1998, musicians and performers entertained the crowd and were part of the catwalk production. The theme was a simple one: a schoolgirl's dream is to become a movie star and play the role of Cleopatra. Drawing parallels between ancient Egypt, punk, and the 1930s, with *trompe l'œil* tattoos and a dress made entirely of safety pins, Galliano produced a show that *Vogue* described as "a spoof of Ancient Egypt as seen through the eyes of Hollywood" and its look as "Cleopatra meets Sid and Nancy."[27] The following year, Galliano produced a catwalk show that drew on Orientalist themes of East as an imaginary place of seduction and eroticism. Titled "The Diorient Express," the show begins with a nineteenth-century steam train arriving at Austerlitz train station. Models disembarked onto a platform stacked with Louis Vuitton travel trunks, dressed in opulent garments with billowing sleeves and colorful headdresses. The models walked languidly amongst the audience who were shaded by palm trees and seated under Berber *souks*, stopping occasionally to pose amongst the baskets of dates and oranges. The show contained a mix of historical references from the European Renaissance to the American West, and was described as a "collision between Pocahontas and Henry VIII."[28] "Whoa there! Stop! Where are we?" wrote Suzy Menkes in the *New York Times*, "Somewhere in the 17th century alongside yet another unlikely fashion heroine: Princess Pocahontas, who marries an Englishman and doffs embroidered doeskin for lace collars, Holbein hats and Renaissance gowns."[29] The gathering of material objects; Berber *souks,* sand, palm trees, and a steam train, removed from their temporal settings, created an illusion of a relation between material objects, place, and time. A colonial setting saved *out* of place and *out* of time.

Oscar Wilde once observed "that the whole of Japan is pure invention. There is no such country. There are no such people."[30] "The Diorient Express" can be seen as an instrument of such inventions. Through the gathering of signs; a souk, palm trees, turbans, an imaginary Orient is invented, along with imaginary taste-makers to accompany them. The show's setting is not arbitrary or consequential but resides in the complex histories and ideological contexts of Western traditions that include the history of representing the "Oriental Other" itself. This complex relationship between the Occident and the Orient is a relationship of power, heavily weighted towards the former. Such power is connected intimately with the construction of knowledge about the Orient, which makes its management easy. "Knowledge gives power, more power requires more knowledge, and so on in an increasingly profitable dialectic of information and control."[31] This knowledge of the Orient incorporates images into Western systems of representation, and in a sense creates the Orient and the Oriental world. "The Oriental is depicted as something one judges (as in a court of law), something one studies and depicts (as in a curriculum), something one disciplines (as in a school or prison), something one illustrates (as in a zoological manual). The point is that, in each case, the Oriental is contained and represented by dominating frameworks."[32]

Sealed, or closed installation

Iris Van Herpen: biomimicry and technology

As we mentioned in the introduction to this book, sealed or closed installations are those works that transport the audience to another place or present the body in unnatural or implausible forms of containment. In 2017, Dutch designer Iris Van Herpen presented her "Aeriform" collection as part of the Fall/Winter couture show in Paris. The collection was a contrast between binaries—water and air, inside and outside, lightness and darkness—and was largely monochrome in color, ranging from stark whiteness to shades of gray. The illusion of the movement of water was reflected in the garments' construction, which contained translucent layering and fabric with rippling patterns. The eighteen garments contained biomorphic elements that explored the body and its surroundings and were informed by Danish underwater artists Between Music. The musicians collaborated with scientists and deep-sea divers to develop oceanic sounds that they then performed on specially built instruments whilst submerged underwater. "Their liquid voices and the subsonic darkness from Between Music overwhelmed me," said Van Herpen, who had the musicians perform on the catwalk as part of her show. "Their work transcends and transforms the conventional and natural relationship between our bodies and the elements." The catwalk was installed in the lower depths of the Cirque d'Hiver in order to capture the darkness and the echoing silence of the deep sea. Five large water tanks were installed on the stage, each chamber contained a musician submerged under the water who sang or played a musical instrument using mini-microphones. Two of the musicians wore garments designed by Van Herpen that moved with the ripples of the green, murky water. Conceptually, the installation bore an eerie resemblance to Alexander McQueen's "Voss" (Spring/ Summer 2001) with its large glass tanks that formed the centerpiece of the show (Figure 17).

While "Voss" contained the fetish writer Michelle Olley, who was arranged naked and covered with moths inside a large class box, the musicians in "Aeriform" resemble water nymphs in Greek mythology trapped inside their watery chambers. This is of no strange fluke of chance, considering that Van Herpen interned at McQueen's atelier after completing studies in fashion design at the ArtEZ Institute of the Arts in Arnhem before starting her own label in 2007. The resemblance between Van Herpen and McQueen does not stop here, but goes even further as the designers have been linked in their ability to push the boundaries of fashion; Van Herpen with her experimental use of three-dimensional technology, and McQueen for his talent in creating a futuristic vision of fashion. In comparing Van Herpen to McQueen, heiress Daphne Guinness, who has collaborated with the designers, says that Van Herpen "has got the same sort of freedom of the imagination, and attention to detail, and getting it done," as McQueen, "She has got this very intellectual mind. There is a singularity to her process. She is monastic, unrelenting."[33] Guinness was referring to the "Crystallization Water Dress," a collaborative project between Van Herpen, Guinness, and Nick Knight of SHOWstudio. In sum, Knight used high-speed cameras to capture water thrown at Guinness, then Van Herpen

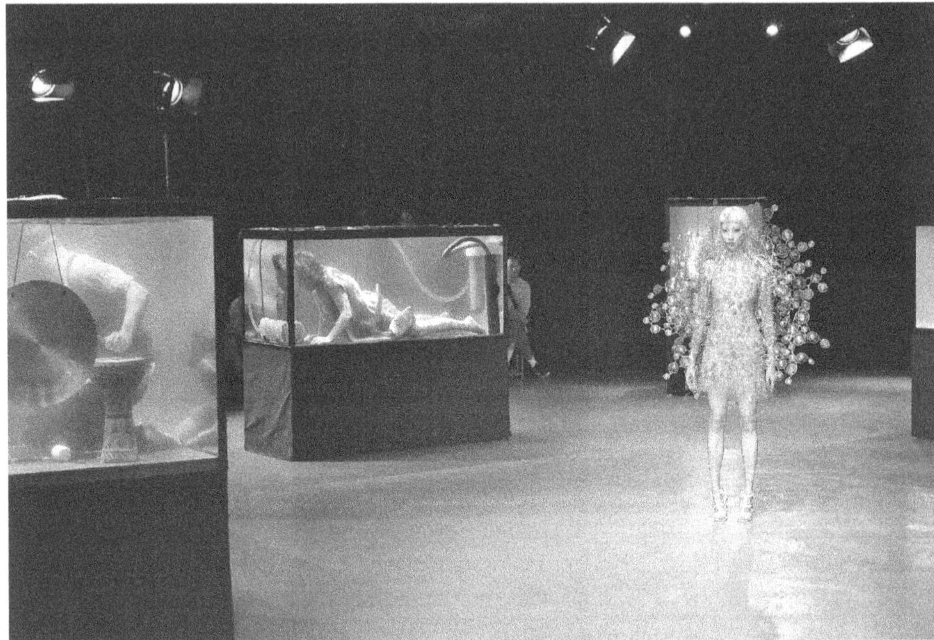

Figure 17 Iris Van Herpen: runway at Paris Fashion Week haute couture, Fall/Winter 2017/2018.

used the imagery to design a couture garment that resembled flowing water. Water and liquid are materials and themes that run through much of Van Herpen's installations. For like liquid that you cannot grasp unless it is contained in a vessel of sorts, "dressing will become something non-material, something that is visible, but not tangible or touchable."[34]

Let us turn back to 2014, to Van Herpen's "Biopiracy" (Fall/Winter ready-to-wear) installation that contained models sealed in clear plastic vacuum-sealed bags suspended above the catwalk. Installed at Les Docks, Cité de la Mode et du Design in Paris, the show was a comment on the human genome project and the theft of the human body via the patenting of genes. The installation was reminiscent of the cult science fiction film *The Matrix* (Wachowski, 1999) that portrays a dystopian future where reality is a simulated machine that uses human bodies as an energy source. Human beings are contained in pods and locked into a dream state, a neuro-interactive virtual reality called the Matrix that convinces them that they are alive and living on earth. Meanwhile, their life source is being sapped through a series of plugs and wires connected to energy towers. As in the Matrix, Van Herpen's models lie in a sealed environment in a state of deep

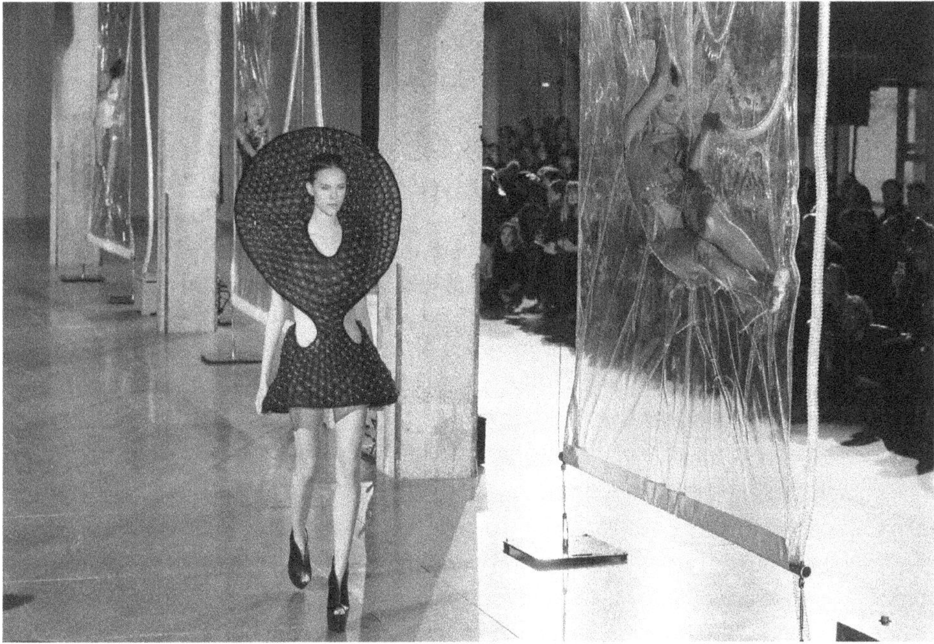

Figure 18 A model presents a creation by Iris Van Herpen during the 2014/2015 Fall/Winter ready-to-wear collection fashion show.

sleep connected by a hose that drains them of their life force (Figure 18). What makes "Aeriform" and "Biopiracy" exemplars of a closed, or sealed, installation is that they place the audience in a darkened setting where they experience their bodies submerged, almost claustrophobically, into a liquid state. In sum, bodies cannot exist in hermetically sealed environments, in water tanks nor vacuum-sealed bags mimicking embryonic sacs. What is so interesting about Van Herpen is that not only is her design practice embedded in experimenting with three-dimensional technologies, her installations tether themes of biomimicry whereby nature is hijacked by new materials and machines.

Alternative realities and new technologies

Since the late 1990s, the rise of new technologies and social media now allows for greater audience participation in fashion shows and events. In 1995, Walter Van Beirendonck used computer-generated images to transform the catwalk into a virtual experience, and ten years later supermodel Kate Moss appeared as a hologram to open an Alexander

McQueen show. In 2009, Victor & Rolf rejected the traditional catwalk and presented their Spring/Summer collection entirely online using only one model. Designers and fashion houses such as Michael Kors, Burberry, and Isaac Mizrahi soon followed suit, preferring to stream their collections on the internet. Then came Alexander McQueen's Spring/Summer 2010 ready-to-wear collection "Plato's Atlantis" that changed the presentation of fashion to a point of no return. Live-streamed on Nick Knight's SHOWstudio.com, the installation, writes Sarah Mower, "crashed through a whole new frontier in the projection of fashion shows as worldwide live entertainment Tuesday night."[35] Where once traditionally fashion was about embodiment, presence, materiality, and real time, it had been displaced into a cinematic dream space.

New technologies allow designers to reach out to a larger audience and market to drive sales. In today's digital landscape, technology is impacting across the fashion industry; from shows being live-streamed and shared on social media, to 24 percent of fashion sales now happening online.[36] Fashion brands are turning their shows into heightened experiences and performances as a direct consumer approach. Social media already enables instant catwalk access, granting audiences who are not present during the event the ability to participate in the performance. In September 2016, California-based virtual reality company Voke partnered with Intel, New York Fashion Week's (NYFW) technical sponsor, to shoot live stereoscopic virtual reality broadcasts that fully immersed audiences into the digital landscape of the catwalk. Audiences can access the experience by downloading wearing Voke's GearVR headset and by downloading Samsung's Gear VR app on their mobile phones. This immersive 2D offering was made available as video-on-demand content for audiences who were unable to watch the shows live. Some of the designers who were using immersive VR technology as part of NYFW 2017 includes the Los Angeles menswear label Band of Outsiders and New York-based Nepalese-American designer Prabal Garung. Meanwhile, Rebecca Minkoff turned to augmented reality by using the shopping app Zeekit, which allows the audience to upload a photograph of themselves wearing garments from Minkoff's collection. As part of Martin Jaarlgard's Spring/Summer 2017 show at London Fashion Week, the audience wore Hololens headsets to watch the collection in the form of a hologram, enabling them to explore the garments from every angle.

As fashion weeks are aimed at reaching a broader audience to generate sales, shows are becoming increasingly focused on attracting the public. For instance, during NYFW 2016 Tommy Hilfiger hosted a two-day fashion-themed carnival complete with food stands, pop-up shops, games, rides, a salon, a tattoo parlor, and a forty-foot Ferris wheel to launch the brand's collaboration with Palestinian-American supermodel Gigi Hadid with the nautical-themed Tommy X Gigi capsule collection (Figure 19). "Tommy Pier" was set up on Pier 16 on South Street Seaport and was Hilfiger's latest venture in what has

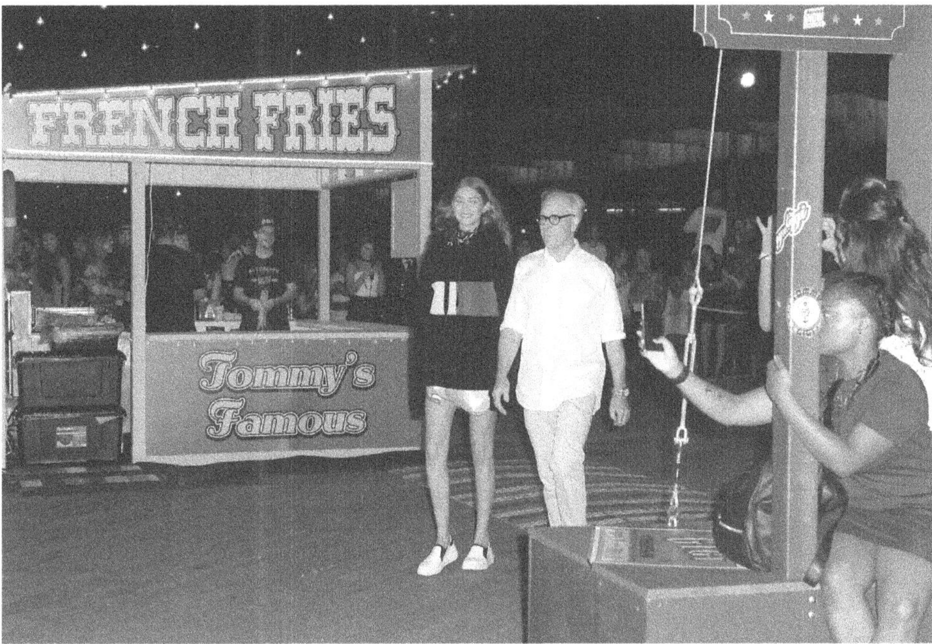

Figure 19 Model Gigi Hadid and designer Tommy Hilfiger walk the runway at the TOMMYNOW Women's Fashion Show during New York Fashion Week at Pier 16 on September 9, 2016 in New York City.

become known as a "consumer-facing runway show," based on a direct-to-consumer model that synchronizes runway shows with retail drops. Two thousand invitations were distributed to Hilfiger customers through the brand's Hilfiger Club to attend the carnival's opening, whilst the carnival remained open for three days for the general public to attend. The show/carnival was live-streamed on the brand's website Tommy.com, and garments were available to purchase via a "see now buy now" business model which has now replaced the traditional fashion system whereby journalists and editors would dictate styles and trends via print media. "See now buy now" enables audiences to watch the show then immediately make purchases, unlike the traditional fashion system, which made garments and collections available six months after the show.

In the past few years, performance art and technology have become inseparable in the presentation of fashion, which has become sophisticated in its context. Fashion is no longer solely about the display of garments, but the concept of the fashion show has become more complex and central to the collection. Fashion brands are now collaborating with multimedia installation artists to create surreal environments that include live artistic tendencies such as performances and happenings. Take, for instance, Riccardo Tisci's Spring/Summer 2016 show for Givenchy. As part of New York Fashion Week, Tisci collaborated with performance artist Marina Abramovic to create a surreal setting that incorporated a diverse assortment of happenings; Serbian folk singers, cellists, violinists, ladders, llamas, a monk, and grand pianos interspersed throughout the space. Like Tommy Hilfiger's riverside setting, Tisci chose Pier 26 in Tribeca as the show's location, which allowed for an unobstructed view of Freedom Tower from every angle. Held on the eve of the anniversary of the September 9/11 terrorist attacks, the show was intended as a mediation on the human losses and a tribute to the people of the city of New York. It was simultaneously to celebrate the opening of the new Givenchy Madison Avenue flagship store. Beginning at dusk, the show opened with a chanting monk whilst performance artists dressed in white shirts and black pants were suspended on platforms against the skyline holding hands and tree saplings, while Abramovic was suspended under faucets of running water that trickled over the audience. Later, as the models paraded down the pier amongst the audience, Abravomic submerged her head under the faucet of water as a gesture of peace and as a symbol of cleansing. A gong sounded the start of the eighty-eight-look show, which included menswear and a series of couture garments from Tisci's past Givenchy couture collections. The multisensory show was a call to slow down, forgive, hope, and love in new beginnings. What made this show such a multisensory event, apart from the multiplatform performances, was that the show used three-dimensional virtual reality technology to record the event. Directed by multimedia artist Marco Brambilla, the film used five cameras to capture all angles and sequences of the fashion show, allowing the audience to experience the event in three-dimensional virtual reality via their computers. Brambilla commented that, "I knew I wanted to immortalize the show and create a kind of time capsule, one that puts you in the center of this incredible universe with as many vantage points as possible."[37] In other words, the catwalk show was an open-ended performance event held in an open space with audience participation, and a film, or sealed, catwalk event, because it maintained cinematic effects and drew the viewer into different worlds using olfactory senses such as touch and smell to transport the view into an imaginary and seductive world. "This show [is] about immersion and experimenting with presence," said Brambilla, "While you are aware you're not physically there, to feel you are is incredible—it places you in that moment in time, at that place."[38]

A sealed, or closed, catwalk show is one during which the audience feels that they are gazing at a different world. The first is more theatrical, such as Gareth Pugh's immersive installation film directed by Ruth Hogben and screened at Uomo Pitti Imaginaire (2011) as part of his collection which was based on religious iconography. The film was screened on the domed ceiling of an eleventh-century Italian basilica, immersing the audience into a mythological world of demi-gods. The closed show also maintains cinematic effects, drawing the viewer into different worlds with the use of olfactory senses such as touch and smell to transport the view into an imaginary and seductive world. Ralph Lauren's immersive four-dimensional experience is a prime example of the convergence of film, cinematic technologies such as green screens, and fashion. To celebrate the brand's historical trajectory, Ralph Lauren used cinematic effects and four-dimensional digital technology to project a film onto the façade of the New York women's flagship store on Madison Avenue. Using screen effects, the film created the illusion of a folding building that opened and closed, transforming into a series of objects including perfume bottles that sprayed scent onto the participating audience. Similarly for the launch of their flagship store in Shanghai, Burberry shipped an entire steam train to the city and projected an interactive film on the exterior of the building that highlighted Burberry heritage and innovation.

Closed fashion shows rely heavily on computer-based imagery and technology to immerse the audience into a virtual space so that they are actively engaged in virtual environments, or digital holographic catwalks. In her chapter "Image: Fashionscapes—Notes Toward an Understanding of Media Technologies and Their Impact on Contemporary Fashion Imagery," Karaminas writes,

> that where once fashion photography, or two dimensional print media, relied on the image to seduce the audience into purchasing a garment by constructing a narrative of desire, digital media *immerses* the audience into the desired world of the luxury brand by evoking visual and olfactory pleasure.[39]

The division between the space of the body and the space of the installation ceases as the lived body becomes one with the space, evoking the concept of totality, or *Gesamtkunstwerk*. Take, for instance, Gareth Pugh's Spring/Summer 2015 for NYFW that featured three short films, *Megalith*, *Chaos*, and *Accession*, alongside a gallery of images that featured Pugh's collection in detail.[40] The "immersive live experience" incorporated eight large LED screens, a live smoking tornado created by artist Daniel Wertzel, and performances by dancers choreographed by Wayne McGregor. For Pugh, the installation "connected the audience with not only the collection itself, but the emotion that went into creating the clothes."[41] For the launch of his Summer/Spring 2015 ready-to-wear Polo womenswear collection, Ralph Lauren created a four-dimensional holographic fashion show that celebrated the opening of his new Polo flagship store in New York. Holographic images of the collection were projected onto a sixty-foot-tall water fountain in Central Park that acted as a backdrop, creating an illusion that the models were floating in space towards the audience. The brand's signature scent, *Pony*, was sprayed into the air, creating a four-dimensional effect, and at the end of the show, a haunting image of Ralph Lauren appeared as an avatar hovering above the Manhattan skyline. Ralph Lauren was not the first fashion brand to take up holographic installations; in 2007, Diesel developed an "L-," and "V-"shaped catwalk that allowed the audience to experience an underwater world. Models strutted down the catwalk accompanied by holographic images of sea creatures and machines floating through space. The eighteen-minute installation was based on Diesel's "Liquid Space" concept for their Spring/Summer 2008 collection and was developed to launch the brand's first perfume. The closed cinematic spaces also belong to the scenes used in fashion films where the body acts as an interloper between worlds. Moving images, or fashion films, enable designers and fashion brands to create an immersive aesthetic, which summarizes their identity or the collection's concept. This narrative style is favored by brands such as Kenzo, Chanel, and Gucci that explore the sartorial heritage of their brand through the medium; others, such as Eckhaus Latta, use found video clips and nature documentaries sliced together in an experimental way.

Fashion film

In some remarks about the establishment of SHOWstudio, Nick Knight expresses his impatience with the still image in its fidelity to the lived, worn garment:

> … it occurred to me that a still image wasn't the best way to show fashion, because designers create pieces of clothing to be seen in movement…. When the Internet came along, it was clear it was a new medium and it could do new things. SHOWstudio came about as both a way to show the process of image-making and a vehicle to facilitate fashion film. It was the vehicle I always wanted to have.[42]

Knight not only goes on to aver that film is the future of the representation of fashion, but that still fashion photography is a thing of the past. "Photography," says Knight, "has to just allow itself to sit down quietly and be the craft it was."[43] But despite Knight's insistence on what he sees as film's fidelity to the mobility of fashion, it should not let us be distracted with other issues of truth. For while the moving image, *ipso facto*, offers the garment in a state of life, it is an illusion that is offered up against myriad digital effects against voids, or in surreal, lunar, or fantasy settings. After the movement of the garment and the movement of the image, the reality stops.

For his Spring/Summer 2018 collection, Pugh rejected the catwalk as a medium, favoring film as an alternative form of display. The attraction to film, argues Pugh, is that "you are able to create an immersive world where people can essentially lose themselves."[44] By combining visuals and sound to create an incredibly powerful, vertiginous experience, the cinematic space can circumvent the creative process and take over the mind. The closed space of the cinema has the ability to transport the audience outside their own comfort zone into unfamiliar places in order to be more receptive to new ideas and concepts. This is achieved by "exposing the viewer to sights, sounds and feelings that are outside of the normal experience, either by making them louder or sharper,"[45] or, as in the case of Pugh's film, *SS18*, more macabre and grotesque. Screened in the closed space of a cinema, the grotesque can evoke the feeling of suffocation and anxiety for the audience. Screened at the British Film Institute's IMAX Theatre (Europe's largest cinema whose screen is the size of four double-decker buses) as part of London Fashion Week, the film was a collaborative project between Nick Knight, performance artist Olivier de Sagazan, choreographer Wayne McGregor, and art director Younji Ku.

As Mikhail Bakhtin describes it, the grotesque is a state of degradation that involves the exaggeration and the glorification of debasement. It always tends to involve parts of the body that protrude, or can be entered, such as the anus, or in the case of Pugh's film, a monstrous vagina in the act of birthing. Unlike the "natural or classical body" of dominant culture, which is considered too "pure" and entirely limited by its boundaries, finished and complete, the grotesque body is a body in reversal; open-ended, boundless, and incomplete. Whereas the "natural" body is domiciled by the civilizing process, the grotesque body (or the "unnatural") is a body in revolt dominated by its primary needs: eating, belching, farting, defecating, copulating, and birthing. Pugh and Knight's film begins with de Sagazan chanting and standing in front of what seems to be a sacrificial plinth laden with food of all sorts. We then see de Sagazan and Pugh seated at a table opposite each other, the table set with a lump of clay and black and red paint. They gradually begin to smear their faces with clay and paint, removing any semblance of human form and molding their heads into "unnatural" creatures in what seems to be a metaphorical crossing over into the dark sphere of demonic existence cast out of the natural world. "Gareth deforms bodies, like me, but with his tools, says de Sagazan, there is that element of science fiction. He speaks of survival. We answer the same question—only our tools, and weapons, diverge."[46] Golems, vampires, and other creatures of the dark, contorting and writhing their bodies in acts of birthing, join them. Later, de Sagazan stands over a clay version of Pugh lying prostrate on a table, his belly swollen and pregnant; de Sagazan leans over Pugh and rips a creature out of his belly "born between feces and urine,"[47] a body born of putrification and decay. The world is turned upside down and in reverse, clay men give birth to unnatural beings, and the sacrilegious becomes the Order.

The short experimental film was inspired by Spanish poet Federico García Lorca's artistic concept of the heightened emotional state of *duende*, the Spanish earth spirit of irrationality and death. According to Lorca, unlike the muse who inspires the artist, the *duende* lies dormant in the artist and is awakened in the artistic quest for authenticity. However, unlike the spirit of exaltation, the *duende* resides in the dark passages and crevices of the artist's emotional state of mind and is called into play in the expression of melancholy, inexplicable sadness, death, and irrationality. It is this heightened awareness of death that drives the artist to creativity. In other words, the *duende* is the spirit of evocation that produces a state of play between the performer and the audience, creating a condition of understanding that allows the intensity of the performance to become endurable. The artist does not succumb willfully to the *duende*, but instead a battle is waged. Lorca identified the *duende* in folk music, especially the flamenco and the Afro-American blues and jazz tradition.[48]

In his performance work, de Sagazan often references the artists Francis Bacon and Antonin Artaud, and he is known for the way in which he uses clay to morph and extend the silhouette of his body, so that the clay becomes one with his flesh. The sixteen-minute film is a disturbing and provocative exploration of the boundaries and spaces of the body as well as a dark vision of the creation of humanity. While the filmic scenes capture the power and spirit of *duende* with all its diabolical leanings, it simultaneously references early mytho-religious beliefs in the creation of humanity from the earth's clay. The Egyptian god Khnum created humans from clay on his potter's wheel, whilst the goddess Hathor breathed life into the clay figures. In Sumerian mythology, the sea goddess Nammu molded humans from clay and brought them to life as a workforce in order to maintain and work the land for the gods. In Christian theology, the Book of Genesis holds that God created Adam (meaning "clay" in Hebrew) from the dust of the earth and breathed into his nostrils the breath of life. The Qur'an also states that Allah created man [sic] from clay by shaping them into human beings and breathing life into their nostrils. But in terms of creation myths and their relevance to Pugh and Knight's film, it is from Greek mythology that it takes its cue. In order to be spared imprisonment for not fighting with the Titans in the war against the Olympians, the Gods charged Prometheus with the task of creating humankind. Prometheus shaped man [sic] out of mud and the goddess (of war and wisdom) Athena breathed life into the clay figure. Prometheus then stole fire from the gods to animate and give people *spirit* and so enabled progress and civilization. "Promethean fire" or "heat" is the substance of life and appears in the film as flames that herald the arrival of a group of writhing dancers dressed in black sheaths printed with flames. The dancers are then replaced by a futuristic vision of women dressed in gold metallic fabric. The choreography and the dancers are "very Baconesque with fractured limbs," writes Wayne McGregor. The dancers' "bodies are in knots, unfolding in an endless, raw, physical behavior, almost possessed and very primal."[49] The film ends with Pugh's Spring/Summer collection worn by models whose eyes are rendered obsolete, digitalized out of existence. The garments they wear consist of architectural protrusions that elongate or widen the body in multiple ways; cage-like constructions and cylindrical shapes that consist of column gowns and sculptural coats in metallic, black, and fire-engine red, morphing the body into something strange and alien altogether.

This is not the first time that Pugh has been drawn to mythological themes and characters to support his collections. His Spring/Summer 2015 collection was informed by pagan rituals in British folklore and included the Padstow Obby Oss, a centuries-old May Day celebration that featured costumed characters referred to as "hobby horses." The celebration begins at midnight on April 30 at the Lion's Inn followed by singing and dancing through the streets by young men dressed in Obb Oss costumes and waving teaser clubs through the air. The men participate in "state-sanctioned" loutish behavior that includes firing pistols and drunken and riotous pranks.[50] Almost one hundred and fifty years ago, C. S. Gilbert, in *The Historical Survey of the County of Cornwall* (1880), notes:

There is an annual jubilee kept up at Padstow, on May 1st, known by the name of the Hobby Horse, in illusion to which, the inhabitants dress up a man in a horse's skin, and lead him through the different streets. This odd looking animal amuses, by many whimsical exploits, the crowd which follows at his heels, particularly by taking up dirty water, wherever it is found, and throwing it into the mouths of his gaping companions. These tricks naturally produce shouts of laughter, and the merriments are accompanied by songs made for the occasion.[51]

Like Pugh's SS18 collection, the presentation of his SS15 collection (which comprised of three short films, Megalith, Chaos, and Accession) drew audience participation into an alternative world by using sight, sound, and space to immerse their senses. As Pugh puts it, "this is about choosing to present the work in a way that hijacks the mind, where the images are expanded to enveloping proportions and connect directly with the depth of feeling behind the work."[52] And like his SS18 collection that connects the audience with the grotesque and the macabre, his SS15 collection is in the spirit of the carnivalesque.

Still installation

Fashion and sex have shared a long and established relationship, which is not surprising given that fashion and sex locate the body as the privileged site of desire. Fashion (like sex) chose the body, a body that has been displayed, a body that has been groomed and paraded, modified and enhanced, through regimes of disciplinary practices, taboos, and transgressions. As an embodied practice, fashion's representational signs are increasingly sexually explicit and suggestive, producing media campaigns and images that display bodies that penetrate and are penetrated, that ejaculate and bleed. Sex, fetish, and horror are themes that have gained salience and prominence in the display of *still* fashion installations, particularly in the development of conceptual exhibitions that cut across art, fashion, and other creative practices. This dialogue between creative practices began in the 1990s when the museum or gallery became an importance space in the display of fashion. As we state in *Fashion and Art* (2012), "designers were drawn closer to artistic practices and conceptual fashion emerged as technology and innovation became key philosophical concerns outweighing the practicality, functionality and wearability of clothing."[53] Multinational corporations such as Pinault-Printemps-Redoute (PPR), Louis Vuitton Moët Hennessey (LVMH), and Verve Clicquot (Ponsardin) came on board as major sponsors of fashion exhibitions, earning considerable profits and in turn aligning their brands with luxury fashion.

In 2015, Veuve Clicquot established the "Widow Series," an immersive art event held each year in London on Halloween to raise money for AIDS research and to honor the Champagne doyenne Barbe-Nicole Ponsardin who was widowed in October 1805, hence *veuve* meaning both "old" and "widow." A different creative team curates the event each year, beginning with Nick Knight's immersive installation, "A Beautiful Darkness." Held in the disused rooms of the old Central St Martins building in Holborn, the installation included six new fashion films, and commissioned work by artists, performers, illustrators, and fashion designers on the theme of horror. Twenty-two fashion illustrations curated by Elli Grace Cummings, stylist and fashion director of *Another Man* magazine, depicted key looks from the Spring/Summer 2016 collection including Givenchy. Perfumer Michael Boadi developed a scent with rose top notes, and artist Rose Robson (whose creative medium is taxidermy) created a range of sculptures from bird skins and wings. As audiences walked through the darkened rooms holding candles, they were greeted by waiting staff dressed in Thom Browne mourning attire, and contorted, grotesque clowns in Gareth Pugh-designed costumes (Figure 20). Knight's house of horror was a site-specific environment that demanded inter-audience interaction as part of the installation. Audience participation had become something of a fashion in contemporary art in the 1990s, but not always with the most sympathetic results. On the other hand, it is a strategy that seems almost natural to fashion. By subjecting the audience to a world of horror, isolated in time and space, and by using the concept of the *Gesamtkunstwerk*, Knight created a fashion installation where all levels of the horror are experienced. "I have curated the show to stimulate all our senses; sight, sound, smell, touch, taste, and also

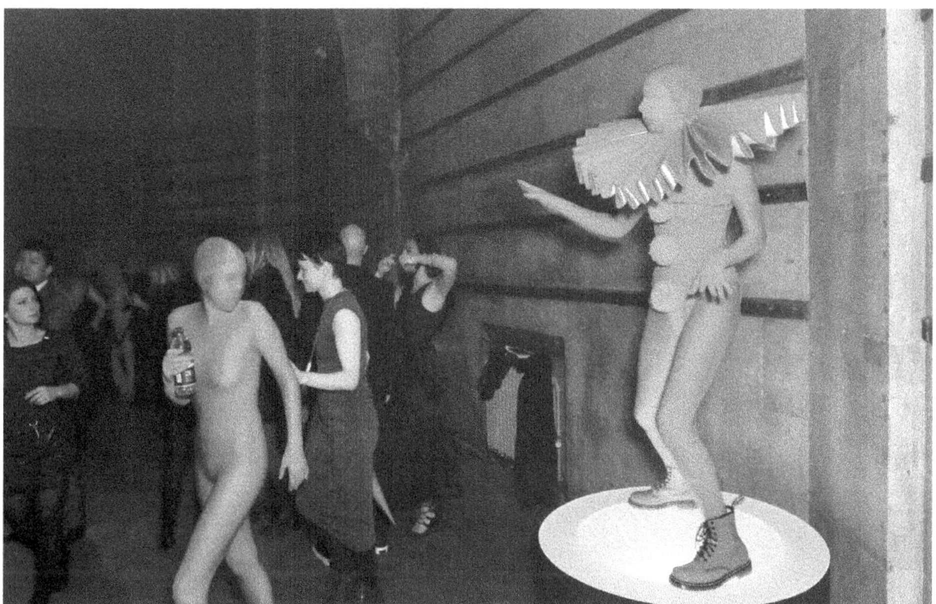

Figure 20 Gareth Pugh's clowns. A general view of the atmosphere at the Veuve Clicquot Widow Series "A Beautiful Darkness" curated by Nick Knight and SHOWstudio on October 28, 2015 in London.

our senses of the paranormal," Knight explained. "I hope A Beautiful Darkness will be a unique cultural event that will offer attendees a new way of seeing fashion and art as well as proposing a beautiful new dark aesthetic to celebrate Halloween."[54] Two years later, in 2017, as part of the Widow Series, former fashion editor of Paris *Vogue*, Corine Roitfeld, and Patrick Kinmouth (once creative director for British *Vogue*) collaborated on "Seven," a fashion installation themed on the seven deadly sins, Wrath, Gluttony, Sloth, Greed, Lust, Pride, and Envy, and referencing the famous crime thriller from 1995. Like "A Beautiful Darkness," "Seven" consisted of a series of seven rooms (each room themed on a sin) over four levels and included garments by Tom Ford, Fendi, Karl Lagerfeld, and Rick Owens. As the audience traversed through the installation, "widow" waitresses dressed in black lace by Tom Ford served Extra Brut Champagne. As a participatory act, the audience was then instructed to throw their glasses over the ledge on the fourth flour, creating a mosaic of crystal shards. While Knight used a disused building to create a house of horrors, Roitfeld and Kinmouth's installation was in an abandoned factory in Islington. The multiple levels and interconnected corridors and staircases created the feeling that audiences were descending into hell (Figure 21). "A Beautiful Darkness" and "Seven"

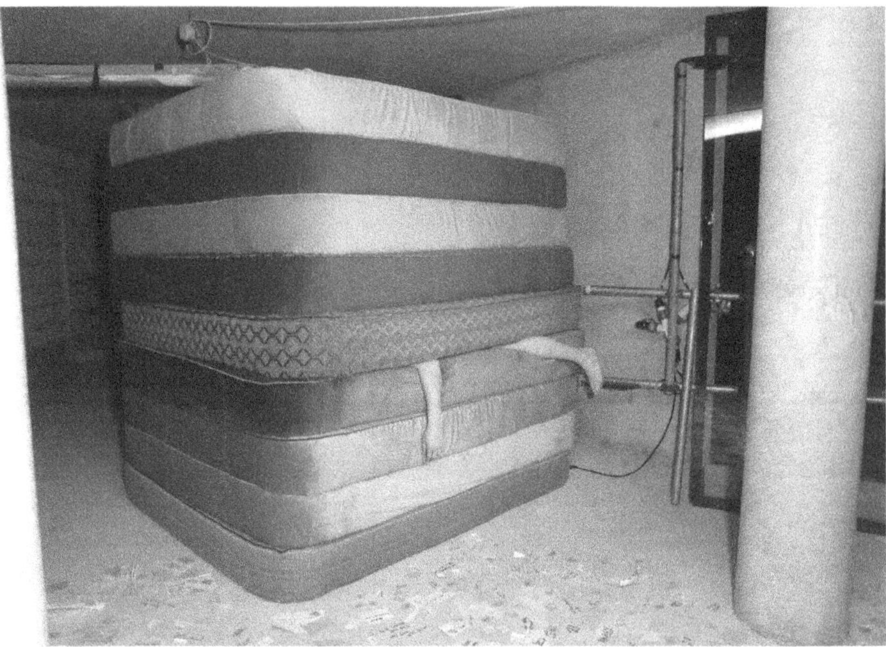

Figure 21 The Veuve Clicquot Widow Series, by Carine Roitfeld and CR Studio LA, 2017, London.

depended on their surroundings to fulfill audience expectations. Once inside the installations, the feelings of horror, fear, and isolation created by the space produce discomfort and a desire to escape. In this way, the audience is *actually installed* in the work. The authorship of the work has now been passed from the curator to the audience.

Still fashion installations take into account the audience's entire sensory field, leaving the concepts of time and space and immersing the audience into the sensory and narrative experience that surrounds them. In his lecture "On the 'Total' Installation," the artist and critic Ilya Kabakow argued that "[One] is simultaneously both a 'victim' and a viewer, who on the one hand surveys and evaluates the installation, and on the other, follows those associations, recollections which arise in him; [sic] he is overcome by the intense atmosphere of the total illusion."[55] This is a very post-, post-post-modern technique, where the viewer is thrust into an other-worldly realm in which critical faculties are suspended.

As part of Art Basel Miami, the Belgian artist Carsten Höller designed a pop-up nightclub for Prada, "The Prada Double Club Miami," that was open for three nights during the fair. The experiential installation included indoor and outdoor spaces that had different identities and functions. Whilst the exterior of the installation contained a lush tropical garden, a dance floor, and a performance area with Caribbean and South African musical acts, the monochromatic interior of the club was located in a former 1920s film studio and contained a moderate ambience that was in juxtaposition to the exterior. Although the audience were guests at the club, enjoying the music and performances, they were also part of the immersive installation. "Each performer embodies the oppositional concept behind the project itself: guests and clubbers can cross permeable boundaries to venture into a double dimension and 'schizophrenic' journey." Höller created the duality of the two oppositional spaces. Holler said that he wanted "guests to feel like they are the only element of color in the monochromatic side that has only greys, blacks and whites, as if a foreign element in a black and white movie— and to feel pale in the hyper-polychromatic other side, where the tropics hit a bit too hard."[56] This was not Muccia Prada's first nightclub commission, nor her first installation. As a long-time patron of the arts, Muccia Prada is familiar with the power that the art world can yield, and in 1993 founded Foundazioni Prada to host cultural programs and support artists. In 2005, Prada commissioned artists Elmgren and Dragset to install a sculpture in the Texan desert near the art town of Marfa to resemble a Prada store with two large windows displaying Prada wear. The permanent sculpture, *"Prada Marfa,"* was intended as a critical intervention into consumer consumption. Similarly, in 2015, Prada commissioned British celebrity artist Damien Hirst to install *"The Juice Bar"* in a tent in the Qatar desert that functioned as a mirage. Also in 2015, Prada asked Rem Koolhass and artist Francesco Vrezoli to create a 1990s-themed party venue for the launch of Prada's diffusion line Miu Miu and the 2016 "Croisière" collection. The Miu Miu Club was a one night only intervention installed in the August Perret-designed Palais d'Iena (1937) in Paris. The installation included a fashion show, dinner, and several musical performance acts. Scaffolding was used to create a series of rooms within a room such as a lounge and a powder room, which later supported a raised catwalk.[57]

When viewed in retrospect, the evolution of fashion's presentation into a multiform spectacle seems natural enough. Fashion as a system as it developed in the eighteenth and nineteenth centuries was always, as Benjamin was keen to remark, about dreams. Fashion and dress since the earliest of times has been about status and belonging, and once in modernity it became available to all, it is not so much the affirmation of legitimate status, but rather its projection as a wish or a promise to both wearer and beholder. Fashion is about the world that was and what could be asserted in a shifting present. In contemporary fashion shows, the narrative that had always been alive in the minds of the participants of fashion is now given scenic physicality. But in uncanny plenty are references to death and the macabre, telling us that fashion is something lived, yet life cannot be fully embraced or understood without death, and that underlining dreams are nightmares. They repel us, but that is part of their fascination and their lure. It is in the echo chambers of deathliness that contemporary fashion continues its lavish, multisensory seduction.

CONCLUSION
FASHION IS A (DIS)EMBODIED PRACTICE, OR, THE PERSISTENCE OF PERFUME

A fundamental, if not the most fundamental, tenet of fashion studies is that it is an embodied practice. Both theoreticians and practitioners return time and again to this principle in order to mark out fashion's differences from art, and from performative practices and qualities elsewhere. Fashion's weddedness to the body is a source of its power, but is also its frailty, since in theory at least it needs a body to bring it to life, and bodies are subject to time in the dynamism of movement, and the transience of life. This logic is built on the simple relationship that borrows from way back to Plato whereby a thing exists as a coupling of an essential, ideal entity and the covering of appearance. The body comes first, is the natural and essential core, and clothing is laid over that.

Now the second tenet of fashion studies is to explore the many conditions and arguments that claim that such logic is errant nonsense. It is by means of the constant friction between these two notions that we are brought to Friedrich Nietzsche, who often claimed that his entire philosophical mission was to overturn Platonism. Whereas Plato wanted to expel all artists from his ideal republic, Nietzsche upheld the artist as the greatest arbiter of humanity, and even an architect of humanity's transition to a new enlightened stage in which appearances were more important than inner essences. After all, essences were invisible while appearances were not. While the problem posed by appearance is that it is not reducible to anything, it is also true that the reducibility of essences is not axiomatic or verifiable; it is but speculation and a matter of blind faith, a faith that, as Nietzsche was wont to argue, has much larger social repercussions. "There would be no life," he writes in *Beyond Good and Evil*, "if it were not wagered on the basis of guesses and appearances." To abolish any consideration of appearances, Nietzsche argues, is to make "truth" redundant.[1] Then comes an audacious flourish which in light of this book is less fanciful than first considered: "Why should the world that preoccupies us not be a fiction?".[2] Our world is shaped through our wishes and our passions, such that our thoughts are just the seemingly reasonable concoctions of our desires and inner impulses. The truth exists somewhere within this unstable environment of projections and hypotheses.

Thus, it is one of the many rewarding insights of Nietzsche's thought that to entrust appearances with the relevance that is their due can be achieved only through a process whereby Plato's philosophy is eternally acknowledged, since to lose it is also to lose knowledge of appearance. One needs to recognize a thing in order to locate the factors, pressures, representations, associations, and so on, that are additive, and that exert themselves on that thing, in order to modify it. It is our fantasy of the anchorage in a stable Cartesian subjectivity that allows us to dress up, perform, adapt, and transform. Barthes calls clothing the signified *par excellence* that is the guarantor of the passage of the body from pure sentience to meaning.[3] Thus in the act of clothing, we deliver ourselves to a state of being. But this being is a meaning subject to countless outward trajectories.

This book has been devoted to the many conditions of fashion's appearance, particularly those conditions that are not circumstance or happenstance, but willfully designed to accompany the garment "itself" such that its meaning is impoverished (or worthless) without it. The purpose of this book is not only to describe a history of the "negative space" of fashion—what exists around the garment—but to suggest a new way of thinking about fashion that moves away from the materiality of the garment to its simultaneous situatedness in imaginary and constructed realms. The French *emplacement* emphasizes the intentionality and self-consciousness of where something is placed. To be fashionable is to be within the zone of other appearances in which one is both a participant and an exemplary figure. Once this is grasped, then it is impossible to return to the seductively simple idea that fashion is contained within the garment. Rather, the garment's coming-to-appearance is always before the garment's physical appearance on the wearer's body.

Fashion installation is where "fashion" is primarily mobilized. This is in the design of stores, in the shape and color of the boxes and bags that deliver it from these stores, it is in the manifold types of images that give the fashion its broader "image." Always transient and contextual, fashion installation places the viewer in an interrogative relation, so that the consumer is made to feel like a participant in an active speculation as to where he or she fits within the particular fashion scenario. This is perhaps why perfume plays such a large part in fashion's life. Coco Chanel's ten percent share in *No. 5* made her a rich woman, and Schiaparelli was saved financially by her own fragrance when Dior and his generation dominated the postwar era. Marcel Rochas is no longer remembered for his gowns but for his fragrance. When we review the roll-call of famous top-end fashion designers, from Tom Ford to Oscar de la Renta to Viktor & Rolf, it is the perfume that is accessible to most people who cannot afford their garments. It is with the perfume that the designer has the most pervasive and widespread "life." And nothing is visible except the spaces in which the wearers of these perfumes perform as fashionable consumers.

While fashion will always be associated with clothing, perhaps the quintessence of fashion is perfume, the "air" that surrounds it, the blooms of seduction and desire that evoke and promise. Perfume requires a body to wear it, and a person to smell it. It is always transient, but because the response to it is through the olfactory nerves, its effects can be the deepest, most sensorially visceral. Installation and performance are both fundamentally transient, instating an event, and thus "eventual." This transience is always a tarrying with death. The relationship of fashion and death is a common, and necessary, philosophical refrain, but also invoked in works by designers themselves. Yet it is this very transience that is also assurance that the liveliness of life is not muted. Installations, performances, and fashions pass, but it is in their passing that a living memory remains.

NOTES

Introduction

1 For a thorough historical and philosophical examination of fashion and representation, see Geczy and Karaminas, *Fashion's Double: The Representation of Fashion in Painting, Photography and Film*, London and New York: Bloomsbury, 2015.

2 Yassana Croizat, "'Living Dolls': François Ier Dresses His Women," *Renaissance Quarterly,* 60(1), Spring 2007, 97. See also Adam Geczy, *The Artificial Body in Fashion and Art: Models, Marionettes and Mannequins*, London and New York: Bloomsbury, 2017.

3 Caroline Evans, *A Mechanical Smile: Modernism and the First Fashion Shows in France and America, 1900–1929*, New Haven and London: Yale University Press, 2013, 58.

4 Michael Fried, "Art and Objecthood," in Gregory Battcock, ed., *Minimal Art: A Critical Anthology*, Berkeley: University of California Press, 1968.

5 Ibid., 128.

6 Julian Rose, "Objects in the Cluttered Field," *October* 140, Spring 2012, 126.

7 This reading of installation as "an activation of space" originates and is explored in detail in the Introduction by Adam Geczy and Benjamin Genocchio, in Geczy and Genocchio, eds., *What Is Installation? Writings on Australian Installation Art*, Sydney: Power Publications, 2001.

8 Mary Kelly, "No Essential Femininity: A Conversation between Mary Kelly and Paul Smith," in *Mary Kelly: Imaging Desire*, Cambridge, MA: MIT Press, 1996, 63.

9 The decentered subject becomes a popular psychoanalytic notion, especially after the writings of Jacques Lacan, who slowly enters the Anglosphere in the late 1960s. Tellingly, the rest of Kelly's comment is as follows: "These are indicated first by the objects and the narrative texts which accompany them; second, by a series of diagrams which refer elsewhere to a kind of explication of the empirical procedures in the work; the third, by another set of diagrams which refer specifically to the work of Lacan and which suggest another possible reading based on psychoanalysis."

10 Rosalind Krauss, *Passages in Modern Sculpture*, Cambridge, MA: MIT Press, 1977, 204.

11 Yvonne Rainer, "A Quasi Survey of Some 'Minimalist' Tendencies in the Quantitatively Minimal Dance Activity Midst the Plethora, or an Analysis of *Trio A*," in Battcock, ed., *Minimal Art*, 269.

12 Ibid., 272.

13 See also Caroline Evans when she introduces her book *The Mechanical Smile* emphasizing that: "It suggests that fashion is also an embodied, four-dimensional practice that exists in both space and time and, therefore, that it is an important, if often overlooked, part of the history of sensibilities as well as of commerce and culture." *A Mechanical Smile: Modernism and the First Fashion Shows in France and America, 1900–1929*, New Haven and London: Yale University Press, 2013, 1.

14 T. J. Clark, *Farewell to an Idea: Episodes from a History of Modernism*, New Haven and London: Yale University Press, 2001, 215.

15 Geczy and Karaminas, *Critical Fashion Practice: From Westwood to Van Beirendonck*, London and New York: Bloomsbury, 2017.

16 By Robert and Richard Sherman.

17 Caroline Evans, *Fashion on the Edge*, New Haven and London: Yale University Press, 2009, 99.

18 See Adam Geczy and Vicki Karaminas, *Critical Fashion Practice from Westwood to Van Beirendonck*, London: Bloomsbury, 2017.

19 Hettie Jones, "What's in a Rick Owens Retrospective? Whatever He Wants," *The New York Times*, https://www.nytimes.com/2017/12/15/fashion/rick-owens-retrospective.html, accessed July 22, 2018.

1 Body: *Mise en scène*

1 Cited in Rhonda Garelick, *Mademoiselle: Coco Chanel and the Pulse of History*, New York: Random House, 2014, 291.

2 Walter Benjamin, *The Arcades Project*, trans. Howard Eiland and Kevin McLaughlin, Cambridge, MA, and London: Belknap/Harvard University Press, 1999, 405.

3 Ibid., 406.

4 Ibid., 389.

5 Eli Friedlander, *Walter Benjamin*, Cambridge, MA: Harvard University Press, 2012, 101–2.

6 Benjamin's enigmatic notion of "awakening" is explained by Alexander Gelley as follows: "What the moment of awakening brings is a sudden awareness of 'the irruption of awakened consciousness,' the sign of the 'what has been.' (*Einfall* signifies to bring to mind, to recall, but also connotes a sudden intrusion or irruption.) For in the dream state the dream self is occluded. Only in the moment of awakening can the self take charge of what the dream has figured forth, recollect it, and make it present. But this moment is fleeting and cannot be claimed as a possession. In another entry, the phenomenon is concentrated in the dialectical image as a lightening flash (*aufblitzendes*) and becomes available only in the 'Now of recognizability' (*Jetzt der Erkennbarkeit*)" (*The Arcades Project*, 473). *Benjamin's Passages: Dreaming, Awakening*, New York: Fordham University Press, 2015, 187.

7 Ibid., 393.

8 Howard Eiland and Michael Jennings, *Walter Benjamin*, Cambridge, MA: Harvard University Press, 2014, 498.

9 Ibid., 492.

10 Alistair O'Neill, "Exhibition: A Display of 'Articles of Clothing for Immediate, Personal, or Domestic Use'—Fashion at the Great Exhibition," in Geczy and Karaminas, eds., *Fashion and Art*, Oxford and New York: Berg, 2012, 190.

11 Amy De La Haye, in Amy De La Haye and Valerie Mendes, *The House of Worth: Portrait of an Archive*, London: V&A Publishing, 2004, 21.

12 Cit. Ibid.

13 Joanne Entwistle, *The Fashioned Body: Fashion, Dress and Modern Social Theory*, Cambridge and Malden, MA: Polity, 2000, 233.

14 Benjamin, *The Arcades Project*, 427.

15 See also Entwistle, who states: "It is apparent that fashion exists not simply as an abstract force or idea, but is *put into practice* through the actions of individual agents, producers, buyers, magazine editors, journalists, retailers and consumers within the various subsections of the fashion system/s. Fashion has to be translated and made meaningful, a process that cuts across economic and cultural practices to the extent that it is impossible to separate the economic from the cultural." *The Fashioned Body*, 235, italics in the original.

16 Ibid., 234.

17 Ibid.

18 Christopher Breward, *The Culture of Fashion*, Manchester and New York: Manchester University Press, 1995, 167.

19 For example, Chicago in 1893 and St. Louis in 1904.

20 See Garelick, *Mademoiselle*, 391.

21 See also the chapter "Display" in Geczy, *Art: Histories, Theories and Exceptions*, Oxford and New York: Berg, 2008, 145–63.

22 Francis Haskell, *The Ephemeral Museum: Old Master Paintings and the Rise of the Art Exhibition*, New Haven and London: Yale University Press, 2000, 45.

23 Robert Jensen, *Marketing the Modern in Fin-de-Siècle Europe*, Princeton, NJ: Princeton University Press, 1994, 112.

24 Ibid.

25 http://www.musee-orangerie.fr/en/article/history-water-lilies-cycle, accessed November 4, 2016.

26 Jan Tchichold, *Commercial Art* (1931), cit. https://thecharnelhouse.org/2014/03/01/el-lissitzkys-soviet-pavilion-at-the-pressa-exhibition-in-cologne-1928/, accessed November 4, 2016, emphasis added.

27 Benjamin Buchloh, "The Dialectics of Design and Destruction: The *Degenerate Art* Exhibition (1937) and the *Exhibition international du Surréalisme* (1938)," *October* 150, "Artists, Designs, Exhibitions Special Issue," Fall, 2014, 57.

28 Ibid., 58.

29 Ibid.

30 Ibid., 59.

31 Claire Grace, "Spoils of the Sign: Group Material's *Americana*, 1985," *October* 150, 139.

32 Created initially in the Anthony d'Offay Gallery, London. See also https://www.centrepompidou.fr/cpv/resource/cLjdb4/rjAaKR

33 Nick Knight, "Thoughts on Fashion Film", SHOWstudio, July 4, 2013, https://www.youtube.com/watch?v=BOBZMS9Bhr0, accessed November 4, 2016.

34 Rosalind Krauss, "Video: The Aesthetics of Narcissism", *October* 1, Spring 1976, 50–64.

35 Ibid., 64.

36 Ibid.

37 Valerie Mendes in De La Haye and Mendes, *The House of Worth*, 39.

38 Benjamin, *The Arcades Project*, 74. See also Evans, *A Mechanical Smile,* 25.

39 As Mary Louise Roberts argues, "By fusing the spirit of the new fashions with this modern consumer ethos of freedom, supporters of fashion were able to present it as liberated and liberating". "Samson and Delilah Revisited: The Politics of Women's Fashion in 1920s France," *The American Historical Review*, 98(3), June 1993, 676.

40 Evans, 30.

41 Michael Barker, "International Exhibitions at Paris Culminating with the Exposition Internationale des Arts et Techniques dans la vie moderne—Paris 1937," *Journal of the Decorative Arts Society 1850–Present*, 27, 2003, 19.

42 Benjamin, *The Arcades Project*, 533.

43 Ibid., 532.

44 Walter Benjamin, "Das Kunstwek im Zeitalter seiner technischer Reproduzierbarkeit," in *Illuminationen*, Frankfurt am Main: Suhrkamp, 1977, 136–69.

45 Mila Ganeva, "Weimar Film as Fashion Show: 'Konfektionskomödien' or Fashion Farces from Lubitsch to the End of the Silent Era," *German Studies Review*, 30(2), May 2007, 290.

46 Ibid.

47 Ibid., 306.

48 Elizabeth Wissinger, *This Year's Model: Fashion, Media, and the Making of Glamour*, New York: New York University Press, 2015, 69.

49 Ibid., 70.

50 Evans, *A Mechanical Smile*, 30.

51 Ibid.

52 As Evans also comments, "Department store shows were staged either in-house on specially built stages or in rented venues, such as theatres and opera houses, although, as Schweitzer argues, the latter option made them vulnerable to appropriation by vaudeville producers". Ibid., 90.

53 Samantha Safer, "Designing Lucile Ltd: Couture and the Modern Interior 1900–1920s," *Journal of the Decorative Arts Society 1850–the Present*, 33, 2009, 41,

54 Cit. ibid.

55 Ibid., 42.

56 Ibid.

57 In the Chicago Rose Room, as Safer adds, "sweeping fabric was hung for curtains, a dressing table placed in the corner was adorned with taffeta and Lucile's trademark floral trim. On the table rested a rounded mirror and personal effects, pictures hung on the paneled walls. Along with the daybed, chairs, and matching bench, low, silk-covered stools were employed for seating". Ibid., 52.

58 Penny Sparke, "The 'Ideal' and the 'Real' Interior in Elsie de Wolf's 'The House in Good Taste' of 1913," *Journal of Design History*, 16(1), 2003, 64.

59 *Portraits intimes du XVIIIe siècle* (Intimate Portraits of the Eighteenth Century, 1857). *La Femme au du XVIIIe siècle* (The Eighteenth Century Woman, 1862), *La du Barry* (On Mme du Barry, 1878), *L'Art du du XVIIIe siècle* (Art of the Eighteenth Century, 1859–1875).

60 Benjamin, "Paris, the Capital of the Nineteenth Century," in *Reflections*, trans. Edmund Jephcott, New York: Schocken, 1978, 154.

61 Sparke, "The 'Ideal' and the 'Real' Interior," 75.

62 Ibid.

63 Joel Kaplan and Shella Stowell, *Theatre and Fashion: Oscar Wilde and the Suffragettes*, Cambridge: Cambridge University Press, 1994, 119.

64 Andrew Bolton, "Response" (to Caroline Evans), in Christopher Breward and Caroline Evans, eds., *Fashion and Modernity*, Oxford and New York: Berg, 2005, 149.

65 Paul Poiret, *En habillant l'epoque*, Paris: Grasset, 1930, 137.

66 Ibid., 138. See also Geczy, *Fashion and Orientalism: Dress, Textiles and Culture from the 17th to the 21st Century*, New York and London; Bloomsbury, 2013, 138–42.

67 Poiret, *En habillant l'epoque*, 138.

68 Ibid., 138–9.

69 Ibid., 139.

70 Ibid.

71 Peter Wollen, "Fashion/Orientalism/The Body," *New Formations*, 1, Spring 1987, 18.

72 Marie Clifford, "Helena Rubenstein's Beauty Salons, Fashion, and Modernist Display," *Winterthur Portfolio*, 38(2/3), Summer/Autumn, 2003, 83.

73 See also ibid.

74 Helena Rubenstein, *My Life for Beauty*, New York: Simon and Schuster, 1966, 38.

75 Clifford, "Helena Rubenstein's Beauty Salons," 90.

76 Ibid., 91.

77 Ibid., 92.

78 Ibid., 102.

79 Cit. Meryle Secrest, *Elsa Schiaparelli*, New York: Knopf, 2014, 19.

80 Ibid., 129.

81 Ibid., 130.

82 Ibid., 136.

83 Ibid., 172–4.

84 Victoria Pass, "Schiaparelli's Convulsive Gloves," in Cristina Giorcelli and Paula Rabinowitz, eds., *Extravagances*, Minnesota: University of Minnesota Press, 2015, 129ff.

85 Ibid., 132.

86 Ibid., 133.

87 Francine Prose, "Elsa Schiaparelli: Le Shocking!," *Aperture*, 176, Fall, 2004, 42.

2 Fashion (almost) without bodies

1 See also Geczy and Karaminas, *Critical Fashion Practice*.

2 Cited in Vivienne Westwood and Ian Kelly, *Vivienne Westwood*, London: Picador, 2014, 144.

3 Ibid.

4 Miles Chapman, "430 King's Road," reproduced in Claire Wilcox, ed., *Vivienne Westwood*, London: V&A Publications, 2004, 36.

5 Ibid., 145.

6 Guy Debord, *La Societé du Spectacle*, Paris: Buchet Chastel, 1967.

7 Westwood and Kelly, *Vivienne Westwood*, 178.

8 John Savage, *The Creation of Youth Culture*, Harmondsworth: Penguin, 2007, xvi; see also Ian Chapman, "Luncheon on the Grass with Manet and Bow Wow Wow: Still Disturbing after All These Years," *Music and Art*, 35(1/2), Spring–Fall, 2010, 95–6.

9 Chapman, ibid., 96.

10 Westwood and Kelly, *Vivienne Westwood*, 164.

11 Ibid.

12 Miles Chapman, in Wilcox, ed., *Vivienne Westwood*, 36.

13 A review in *Artforum* (December 1995), fashion magazine *Visionaire* (no. 17).

14 For example, Caroline Evans, in Caroline Evans and Susannah Frankel, *The House of Viktor & Rolf*, exh. cat. Barbican Centre, London and New York: Merrell, 2008, 12.

15 Cit. http://www.basenotes.net/ID26123491.html

16 Bonnie English, *Japanese Fashion Designers: The Work and Influence of Issey Miyake, Yohgi Yamamoto and Rae Kawakubo*, London: Bloomsbury, 2011, 159.

17 Viktor & Rolf, cited in Angel Chang, "Viktor and Rolf," in Valerie Steele, ed., *The Berg Companion to Fashion*, Oxford: Berg, 2010, 710.

18 Caroline Evans, *Fashion at the Edge*, New Haven and London: Yale University Press, 2009, 93.

19 See also http://bombmagazine.org/article/2606/santiago-sierra

20 Heinrich von Kliest, "Über das Marionettentheater" (1810), *Sämtliche Werke*, Leipzig: Im Insel Verlag, n.d. See also Geczy, *The Artificial Body in Fashion and Art*, 6, 54–60.

21 Ibid.

22 See also Evans, *Fashion on the Edge*, 166ff.

23 http://www.indexmagazine.com/interviews/viktor_and_rolf.shtml, accessed November 21, 2016.

24 See Jane Mulvagh, "FASHION/Modes of resistance: in late 1944 Paris was free, but the fashion industry was in tatters. A unique artistic collaboration helped to re-establish French couture. Its heroes were 70cm tall," *Independent*, July 31, 1994, http://www.independent.co.uk/arts-entertainment/fashion-modes-of-resistance-in-late-1944-paris-was-free-but-the-fashion-industry-was-in-tatters-a-1418052.html, accessed November 23, 2016; Secrest, *Schiaparelli*, 292–5.

25 Lauren Le Rose, "Dutch Design Guru's Viktor and Rolf bring their 'Dolls' Collection to the Royal Ontario Museum for Luminato," Style, *National Post*, April 9, 2013: 'http://news.nationalpost.com/life/dutch-design-gurus-viktor-rolf-bring-their-dolls-collection-to-the-royal-ontario-museum-for-luminato, accessed November 18, 2015.

26 Interview with Susanna Frankel, in Caroline Evans and Frankel, eds., *The House of Viktor & Rolf*, London: Merrell Publishers and the Barbican Gallery, 2008, 23.

27 Ibid., 24.

28 Cate Trotter, "50 Most Beautiful Concept Stores in the World," https://www.linkedin.com/pulse/50-most-beautiful-concept-stores-world-cate-trotter/. accessed January 15, 2018.

29 Elizabeth Patton and Vanessa Friedman, "Colette Fashion Destination Paris, is to Close in December, July 12, 2017," Fashion and Style, *New York Times*, https://www.nytimes.com/2017/07/12/fashion/colette-paris-sarah-andelman.html, accessed January 21, 2018.

30 Sara Bauknecht, "Big Apple Bound for the Holidays? Dover Street Market New York is a Must-See Shopping Destination," http://www.post-gazette.com/life/fashion/2017/11/13/Dover-Street-Market-New-York-shopping-destination-NYC-Comme-des-Garcons/stories/201711120012, accessed January 23, 2017.

31 Marcy Medina, "Hermes Opens Final 'Hermesmatic' Pop Up at Westfield Century City," http://wwd.com/fashion-news/fashion-scoops/hermes-opens-final-hermesmatic-pop-up-at-westfield-century-city-11048056/, accessed November 24, 2018.

32 Patrizia Calefato, *Fashion, Time, Language*, Balti Moldova: Editions Universitaires Europeennes, 2017, 39.

33 Calefato, Fashion, 39.

34 Calefato, Fashion, 39.

35 https://www.ranker.com/list/best-luxury-fashion-brands/ranker-shopping, accessed February 1, 2018.

36 Otto Riewoldt, ed., *Brandscaping: Worlds of Experience in Retail Design*, Boston and Berlin: Berhauser Verlag AG, 2002.

37 Otto Riewoldt, *Retail Design*, New York: Nte Neues, 2000, 38.

38 The Ralph Lauren Corporation includes products in four categories: apparel, home, accessories, and fragrances. Brand labels include Ralph Lauren Purple Label, Ralph Lauren Collection, Double RL, RLX, American Living, Lauren Ralph Lauren, Polo Ralph Lauren, Polo Ralph Lauren Children's, Ralph Lauren Home, Chaps and Club Monaco.

39 D. J. Huppatz and Veronica Manlow, "Producing and Consuming American Mythologies: Branding in Mass Market Fashion Firm," in *Global Fashion Brands: Style, Luxury and History*, ed. Joseph Hancock II, Gjoko Muratovski, Veronica Manlow, and Anne Pierson Smith, Bristol: Intellect, 2014, 23–40.

40 David Kamp, "London Swings Again," *Vanity Fair*, February 7, 2007, https://www.vanityfair.com/magazine/1997/03/london199703, accessed 8 February, 2018.

41 Seth Ambramovitch, "Paul Smith Boutique Partners with Instagram on Rainbow Stripes for L.A Pride," https://www.hollywoodreporter.com/news/paul-smiths-pink-boutique-unveils-rainbow-stripes-la-pride-1008273, accessed February 8, 2018.

42 Leah Chernikoff, "Chanel's Supermarket Sweep," https://www.elle.com/fashion/news/a19050/chanel-fall-2014-runway-show-supermarket-decor/, accessed July 22, 2018.

43 William H. Meyers, "Maxim's Is the Name of the Game," *The New York Times*, http://www.nytimes.com/1987/05/03/magazine/maxim-s-name-is-the-game.html?pagewanted=all, accessed February 18, 2018

44 Frank J. Prial, "Maxim's the Paris Restaurant Is Sold to Cardin Enterprises," *The New York Times*, http://www.nytimes.com/1981/05/06/garden/maxim-s-the-paris-restaurant-is-sold-to-cardin-enterprises.html, accessed February 16, 2018.

45 William H. Meyers, "Maxim's Is the Name of the Game," *The New York Times*, http://www.nytimes.com/1987/05/03/magazine/maxim-s-name-is-the-game.html?pagewanted=all, accessed February 18, 2018.

46 Licensing agreements between Pierre Cardin and Maxim's restaurant included a diffusion label and over eight hundred licensees selling nine hundred products, including homewares in ninety-three countries.

47 Pierre Bourdieu, "Distinction: A Social Critique of the Judgement of Taste," in Carole Counihan and Penny Van Esterick, eds., *Food and Culture: A Reader*, third edition, New York and London: Routledge, 2013.

48 Norbert Elias, *The Civilizing Process, The History of Manners*, Oxford: Blackwell, 1969.

49 Sara Lighthall, "Why Food Is Less about the Tag and More about the Experience," taghttps://relate.zendesk.com/articles/foodporn-less-about-tag-more-about-experience/. accessed February 23, 2018.

50 Geoff Williams, "How Millennials Will Shape Food in 2017," https://www.forbes.com/sites/geoffwilliams/2016/12/31/how-millennials-will-shape-food-in-2017/#5cd004e26a6d, accessed February 22, 2018.

3 Body-in-space and the *Gesamtkunstwerk*

1 Karl Friedrich Eusebius Trahndorff, *Ästhetik oder Lehre von Weltanschauung und Kunst*, 2 vols, Berlin, 1827.

2 "Die Kunst und die Religion" (Art and Religion, 1849), "Das Kunstwerk der Zukunft" (The Work of Art of the Future, 1849), "Oper und Drama" (Opera and Drama, 1852).

3 Cited in Wolf Gerhard Schmidt, "Was ist ein 'Gesamtkunstwerk'? Zur medienhistorischen Neubestimmung des Begriffs", *Arvhiv für Musikwissenschaft*, 68(2), 2011, 160.

4 "Jede Einzelkunst kann heutzutage nichts Neues Erfinden," Richard Wagner, *Sämtliche Schriften und Dichtungen*, Leipzig: Breitkopf & Härtel, 1848–1926, v. 12, 269.

5 See also Ursula Rehn Wolfman, "Richard Wagner's Concept of the '*Gesamtkunstwerk*'," *Interlude*, March 12, 2013, http://www.interlude.hk/front/richard-wagners-concept-of-the-gesamtkunstwerk/, accessed November 24, 2016.

6 Carolyn Birdsall, *Sound, Technology and Urban Space in Germany, 1933–1945*, Amsterdam: Amsterdam University Press, 2012, 143.

7 Ibid., 145.

8 Ibid., 157.

9 Ibid., 162.

10 Julia Cloot, "Züge eines Gesamtkunstwerks? Richard Wagner und das Aktuelle Musiktheater," *Neue Zeitschrift für Musik (1991–)*, 174(1), 2013, 29–31.

11 Ibid., 33.

12 Annette Michelson, "'Where Is Your Rupture?': Mass Culture and the Gesamtkunstwerk," *October* 56, Spring 1991, 58.

13 Cited in Susannah Frankel, "Introduction," in Andrew Bolton, ed., *Alexander McQueen: Savage Beauty*, New Haven, London, and New York: Yale University Press and the Metropolitan Museum of Art, 2011, 24.

14 Ibid., 22.

15 Andrew Bolton, "Preface" in ibid., 12.

16 Cited in Bolton, ibid.

17 See Geczy, *Artificial Bodies*, 73–5.

18 See also "Long Love McQueen", http://the-widows-of-culloden.tumblr.com/post/58537891727/alexander-mcqueen-ss-1997-la-poupee-the, accessed December 27, 2016.

19 Julie Wosk comments of McQueen's outfitting of Mullins as follows: "McQueen's 1999 fashion ensembles for Mullins, though, were paradoxically freeing and confining. In the 2011 blockbuster exhibit of McQueen's fashions, *Alexander McQueen: Savage Beauty*, held at the Metropolitan Museum of Art in New York, a mannequin was dressed in one of the designer's creations made for Mullins: a corset of brown leather, skirt of cream silk lace, and custom-made prosthetic legs with floral motifs carved from wood. The sections of the corset were

pieced together with enlarged stitches resembling the Bride of Frankenstein's pieced-together frame, but the layered lace skirt softened the look. As the ensemble suggests, McQueen himself took on the role of Frankenstein." *Female Robots, Androids, and Other Artificial Eves*, New Brunswick: Rutgers University Press, 2015, 173.

20 Stephen Seely, "How Do You Dress a Body without Organs? Affective Fashion and Nonhuman Becoming," *Women's Studies Quarterly*, 41.2, Spring/Summer, 2012, 253.

21 Evans, *Fashion at the Edge*, 98.

22 Ibid., 102.

23 Michael Specter, "Le Freak C'est Chic," *The Guardian,* https://www.theguardian.com/theobserver/2003/nov/30/features.magazine47, accessed November 23, 2017.

24 Ginger Gregg Duggan, "The Greatest Show on Earth: A Look at Contemporary Fashion Shows and Their Relationship to Performance Art," in *Fashion Theory*, Volume 5, Issue 3, 250.

25 Caroline Evans, *Fashion at the Edge*, New Haven and London: Yale University Press, 2003, 26.

26 https://www.youtube.com/watch?v=UxOuOMcNvSU, accessed June 1, 2018.

27 Laird Borrelli-Persson, "John Galliano Fall 1997 Ready-to-Wear, Runway, Vogue," https://www.vogue.com/fashion-shows/fall-1997-ready-to-wear/john-galliano, accessed November 15, 2017.

28 Ginger Gregg Duggan, "The Greatest Show on Earth: A Look at Contemporary Fashion Shows and Their Relationship to Performance Art," in *Fashion Theory*, Volume 5, Issue 3, 249.

29 Suzy Menkes, "Galliano's Diorient Express Runs Out of Steam," *The New York Times*, http://www.nytimes.com/1998/07/21/style/gallianos-diorient-express-runs-out-of-steam.html, accessed November 28, 2017.

30 Oscar Wilde, "The Decay of Lying," in H. Adams, ed., *Critical Theory since Plato*, New York: Harcourt Brace, 1992, 684.

31 Edward W. Said, *Orientalism: Western Conceptions of the Orient*, London: Penguin, 1978, 36.

32 Ibid., 30.

33 Rebecca Mead, "Iris Van Herpen's High Tech Couture," *The New Yorker,* https://www.newyorker.com/magazine/2017/09/25/iris-van-herpens-hi-tech-couture, accessed July 10, 2018.

34 The "Water-Dress," Biomimicry by Iris Van Herpen, Promystyl Blog, International Style and Trend Office, http://www.promostyl.com/blog/en/the-water-dress-by-iris-van-herpen/, accessed July 10, 2018.

35 Sarah Mower, https://www.vogue.com/fashion-shows/spring-2010-ready-to-wear/alexander-mcqueen, accessed January 8, 2018.

36 Samira Hersom, "Tech on the Runway: An Interview with Jenico Preston, BFC Commercial Director," nomomagnews.com/blog/2017/11/18/tech-on-the-runway-an-interview-with-jenico-preston-bfc-commercial-director, accessed November 26, 2017.

37 Gillian Sagansky, "Capturing the Elusive Givenchy Spring 2016 Show," *W Magazine* online, https://www.wmagazine.com/story/givenchy-spring-2016-marco-brambilla, accessed December 10, 2017.

38 Ibid.

39 Vicki Karaminas, "Image: Fashionscapes—Notes Toward an Understanding of Media Technologies and Their Impact on Contemporary Fashion Imagery," in Geczy and Karaminas eds., *Fashion and Art*, 180.

40 For a detailed analysis of Pugh's immersive installation, see Geczy and Karaminas, "Gareth Pugh's Corporeal Uncommensurabilities," in *Critical Fashion Practice from Westwood to Van Beirendonck*, London: Bloomsbury, 2017, 45–55.

41 Gareth Pugh, Spring/Summer 2015, Showstudio. https://www.youtube.com/watch?v=qeaXJhQyjAI

42 Nick Knight and Diane Smith, "Nick Knight: Showman—An Interview with Diane Smith," *Aperture*, 197, Winter 2009, 74.

43 Ibid.

44 Hannah Tindle, Nick Knight, and Gareth Pugh on the Future of Fashion, Dazed, http://www.dazeddigital.com/fashion/article/37426/1/gareth-pugh-and-nick-knight-on-the-future-of-fashion-film-ss18, accessed January 6, 2018.

45 Natasha Bird, "Gareth Pugh Stages Radical Fashion Film at the BFI IMAX during London Fashion Week SS18," http://www.elleuk.com/fashion/trends/news/a38640/gareth-pugh-stages-radical-fashion-film-at-the-imax/, accessed January 8, 2018.

46 Charlotte Gush, "Gareth Wants to Hijack Your Mind with His Visceral Anti-Fashion Film, i-D," https://i-d.vice.com/en_uk/article/7xkvpd/gareth-pugh-wants-to-hijack-your-mind-with-his-visceral-anti-fashion-film, accessed January 5, 2018.

47 Georges Bataille, *Eroticism, Death and Sexuality*, trans. Mary Dalewood, San Francisco: City Lights Books, 1957, 58.

48 Federico García Lorca, *Theory and Play of the Duende*, trans. A. S. Kline, 2007, http://www.poetryintranslation.com/PITBR/Spanish/LorcaDuende.php, accessed January 14, 2018.

49 Jerry Stafford, "Presenting Gareth Pugh's Vision for Spring/Summer 2018," *Vogue*, http://www.vogue.co.uk/article/gareth-pughs-springsummer-2018-film, accessed January 8, 2018.

50 See the book chapter "Gareth Pugh's Corporeal Uncommensurabilities," in Adam Geczy and Vicki Karaminas, *Critical Fashion Practice from Westwood to Van Beirendonck*, London: Bloomsbury, 2017.

51 The Padstow Obby Oss, https://padstowobbyoss.wordpress.com/about/, accessed January 10, 2018.

52 Natasha Bird, "Gareth Pugh Stages Radical Fashion Film at the BFI IMAX during London Fashion Week SS18," http://www.elleuk.com/fashion/trends/news/a38640/gareth-pugh-stages-radical-fashion-film-at-the-imax/, accessed January 10, 2018.

53 Adam Geczy and Vicki Karaminas, *Fashion and Art*, Oxford: Berg, 9.

54 www.nickknight.com, accessed January 12, 2018.

55 Kabakov, Ilya, *On the "Total" Installation*, Ostfildern, Germany: Cantz, 1995, 243–60.

56 Alice Harrison, "Carsten Höller Creates a Pop Up Club for Prada," https://www.ignant.com/2017/12/13/carsten-holler-creates-a-pop-up-nightclub-for-prada/, accessed January 15, 2018.

57 For a more detailed critical analysis of Miuccia Prada's collaborative relationship with the arts, see the chapter "Miuccia Prada's Industrial Materialism," in Adam Geczy and Vicki Karaminas, *Critical Fashion Practice: From Westwood to Van Beirendonck*, London: Bloomsbury, 2017, 61–76.

Conclusion

1 Friedrich Nietzsche, *Jenseits von Gut und Böse*, in *Werke*, Salzburg: Verlag Das Bergland-Buch, 1985, 4: 179.

2 Ibid., 180.

3 Roland Barthes, *The Fashion System*, trans. Matthew Ward and Richard Howard, Berkeley and London: California University Press, 1990, 258.

BIBLIOGRAPHY

Ambramovitch, Seth. "Paul Smith Boutique Partners with Instagram on Rainbow Stripes for LA Pride," https://www.hollywoodreporter.com/news/paul-smiths-pink-boutique-unveils-rainbow-stripes-la-pride-1008273. Accessed February 8, 2018.

Barker, Michael. "International Exhibitions at Paris Culminating with the Exposition Internationale des Arts et Techniques dans la vie moderne—Paris 1937," *Journal of the Decorative Arts Society 1850–Present*, 27, 2003, 6–21.

Barthes, Roland. *The Fashion System*, trans. Matthew Ward and Richard Howard, Berkeley and London: California University Press, 1990.

Bataille, Georges. *Eroticism, Death and Sexuality*, trans. Mary Dalewood, San Francisco: City Lights Books, 1957.

Battcock, Gregory, ed. *Minimal Art: A Critical Anthology*, Berkeley: University of California Press, 1968.

Bauknecht, Sara. "Big Apple Bound for the Holidays? Dover Street Market New York is a Must-See Shopping Destination," http://www.post-gazette.com/life/fashion/2017/11/13/Dover-Street-Market-New-York-shopping-destination-NYC-Comme-des-Garcons/stories/201711120012. Accessed January 23, 2017.

Benjamin, Walter. *Illuminationen*, Frankfurt am Main: Suhrkamp, 1977.

Benjamin, Walter. *Reflections*, trans. Edmund Jophcott, New York: Schocken, 1978.

Benjamin, Walter. *The Arcades Project*, trans. Howard Eiland and Kevin McLaughlin, Cambridge, MA, and London: Belknap/Harvard University Press, 1999.

Bird, Natasha. "Gareth Pugh Stages Radical Fashion Film at the BFI IMAX during London Fashion Week SS18," http://www.elleuk.com/fashion/trends/news/a38640/gareth-pugh-stages-radical-fashion-film-at-the-imax/. Accessed January 8, 2018.

Birdsall, Carolyn. *Sound, Technology and Urban Space in Germany, 1933–1945*, Amsterdam: Amsterdam University Press, 2012.

Bolton, Andrew, ed. *Alexander McQueen: Savage Beauty*, New Haven, London, and New York: Yale University Press and the Metropolitan Museum of Art, 2011.

Bourdieu, Pierre. "Distinction: A Social Critique of the Judgement of Taste," in Carole Counihan and Penny Van Esterick, eds. *Food and Culture: A Reader*, third edition, New York and London: Routledge, 2013.

Breward, Christopher. *The Culture of Fashion*, Manchester and New York: Manchester University Press, 1995.

Breward, Christopher and Caroline Evans, eds. *Fashion and Modernity*, Oxford and New York: Berg, 2005.

Buchloh, Benjamin. "The Dialectics of Design and Destruction: The *Degenerate Art* Exhibition (1937) and the *Exhibition international du Surréalisme* (1938)," October, 150, "Artists, Designs, Exhibitions: Special Issue," Fall, 2014, 49–62.

Calefato, Patrizia. *Fashion, Time, Language*, Balti Moldova: Editions Universitaires Europeannes, 2017.

Chapman, Ian. "Luncheon on the Grass with Manet and Bow Wow Wow: Still Disturbing after All These Years," *Music and Art*, 35(1/2), Spring/Fall, 2010, 95–104.

Chernikoff, Leah. "Chanel's Supermarket Sweep," https://www.elle.com/fashion/news/a19050/chanel-fall-2014-runway-show-supermarket-decor/ Accessed July 22, 2018.

Clark, T. J. *Farewell to an Idea: Episodes from a History of Modernism*, New Haven and London: Yale University Press, 2001.

Clifford, Marie. "Helena Rubenstein's Beauty Salons, Fashion, and Modernist Display," *Winterthur Portfolio*, 38(2/3), Summer/Autumn, 2003, 83–108.

Cloot, Julia. "Züge eines Gesamtkunstwerks? Richard Wagner und das Aktuelle Musiktheater," *Neue Zeitschrift für Musik (1991–)*, 174(1), 2013, 28–33.

Croizat, Yassana. "'Living Dolls': François Ier Dresses His Women," *Renaissance Quarterly*, 60(1), Spring 2007.

Debord, Guy. *La Societé du Spectacle*, Paris: Buchet Chastel, 1967.

De La Haye, Amy and Valerie Mendes. *The House of Worth: Portrait of an Archive*, London: V&A Publishing, 2004.

Duggan, Ginger Gregg. "The Greatest Show on Earth: A Look at Contemporary Fashion Shows and Their Relationship to Performance Art," *Fashion Theory*, 5(3), 243–70.

Eiland, Howard and Michael Jennings. *Walter Benjamin*, Cambridge, MA: Harvard University Press, 2014.

Elias, Norbert. *The Civilizing Process*, Vol: *The History of Manners*, Oxford: Blackwell, 1969.

English, Bonnie. *Japanese Fashion Designers: The Work and Influence of Issey Miyake, Yohgi Yamamoto and Rae Kawakubo*, London: Bloomsbury, 2011.

Entwistle, Joanne. *The Fashioned Body: Fashion, Dress and Modern Social Theory*, Cambridge and Malden, MA: Polity, 2000.

Evans, Caroline. *Fashion at the Edge*, New Haven and London: Yale University Press, 2009.

Evans, Caroline. *A Mechanical Smile: Modernism and the First Fashion Shows in France and America, 1900–1929*, New Haven and London: Yale University Press, 2013.

Evans, Caroline and Susannah Frankel, eds. *The House of Viktor & Rolf*, London: Merrell Publishers and the Barbican Gallery, 2008.

Friedlander, Eli. *Walter Benjamin*, Cambridge, MA: Harvard University Press, 2012.

Galley, Alexander. *Benjamin's Passages: Dreaming, Awakening*, New York: Fordham University Press, 2015.

Ganeva, Mila. "Weimar Film as Fashion Show: 'Konfektionskomödien' or Fashion Farces from Lubitsch to the End of the Silent Era," *German Studies Review*, 30(2), May 2007, 288–310.

Garelick, Rhonda. *Mademoiselle: Coco Chanel and the Pulse of History*, New York: Random House, 2014.

Geczy, Adam. *Fashion and Orientalism: Dress, Textiles and Culture from the 17th to the 21st Century*, New York and London: Bloomsbury, 2013.

Geczy, Adam. *The Artificial Body in Fashion and Art: Models, Marionettes and Mannequins*, London and New York: Bloomsbury, 2017.

Geczy, Adam and Benjamin Genocchio, eds. *What Is Installation? Writings on Australian Installation Art*, Sydney: Power Publications, 2001.

Geczy, Adam and Vicki Karaminas, eds. *Fashion and Art*, Oxford and New York: Berg, 2012.

Geczy, Adam and Vicki Karaminas. *Fashion's Double: The Representation of Fashion in Painting, Photography and Film*, London and New York: Bloomsbury, 2015.

Geczy, Adam and Vicki Karaminas. *Critical Fashion Practice: From Westwood to van Beirendonck*, London and New York: Bloomsbury, 2017.

Giorcelli, Cristina and Paula Rabinowitz, eds. *Extravagances*, Minnesota: University of Minnesota Press, 2015.

Gordon, Beverly. "Woman's Domestic Body: The Conceptual Conflation of Women and Interiors in the Industrial Age," *Winterthur Portfolio*, 31(4), 1996, 281–301.

Grace, Claire. "Spoils of the Sign: Group Material's *Americana*, 1985," *October* 150, "Artists Designs Exhibitions Special Issue," Fall, 2014, 133–60.

Gush, Charlotte. "Gareth Wants to Hijack Your Mind with His Visceral Anti-Fashion Film, i-D," https://i-d.vice.com/en_uk/article/7xkvpd/gareth-pugh-wants-to-hijack-your-mind-with-his-visceral-anti-fashion-film. Accessed January 5, 2018.

Harrison, Alice. "Carsten Höller Creates a Pop-Up Club for Prada," https://www.ignant.com/2017/12/13/carsten-holler-creates-a-pop-up-nightclub-for-prada/. Accessed January 15, 2018.

Haskell, Francis. *The Ephemeral Museum: Old Master Paintings and the Rise of the Art Exhibition*, New Haven and London: Yale University Press, 2000.

Hersom, Samira. "Tech on the Runway: An Interview with Jenico Preston, BFC Commercial Director," nomomagnews.com/blog/2017/11/18/tech-on-the-runway-an-interview-with-jenico-preston-bfc-commercial-director. Accessed November 26, 2017.

Huppatz, D. J. and Veronica Manlow. "Producing and Consuming American Mythologies: Branding in Mass Market Fashion Firm," in *Global Fashion Brands: Style, Luxury and History*, ed. Joseph Hancock II, Gjoko Muratovski, Veronica Manlow, and Anne Pierson Smith, Bristol: Intellect, 2014.

Jensen, Robert. *Marketing the Modern in Fin-de-Siècle Europe*, Princeton, NJ: Princeton University Press, 1994.

Kabakov, Ilya. *On the "Total" Installation*, Ostfildern, Germany: Cantz, 1995, 243–60.

Kamp, David. "London Swings Again," *Vanity Fair*, February 7, 2007, https://www.vanityfair.com/magazine/1997/03/london199703. Accessed February 8, 2018

Kaplan, Joel and Shella Stowell. *Theatre and Fashion: Oscar Wilde and the Suffragettes*, Cambridge: Cambridge University Press, 1994.

Karaminas, Vicki. "Image: Fashionscapes—Notes Toward an Understanding of Media Technologies and Their Impact on Contemporary Fashion Imagery," in *Fashion and Art*, ed. Adam Geczy and Vicki Karaminas, Oxford: Berg, 2012.

Kelly, Mary. *Mary Kelly: Imaging Desire*, Cambridge, MA: MIT Press, 1996.

Kleist, Heinrich von. "Über das Marionettentheater," *Sämtliche Werke* (1810), Leipzig: Im Insel Verlag, n.d.

Knight, Nick. "Thoughts on Fashion Film," SHOWstudio, July 4, 2013, https://www.youtube.com/watch?v=BOBZMS9Bhr0

Knight, Nick and Diane Smith. "Nick Knight: Showman—An Interview with Diane Smith," *Aperture*, 197, Winter 2009, 68–75.

Krauss, Rosalind. "Video: The Aesthetics of Narcissm," *October* 1, Spring 1976: 50–64.

Krauss, Rosalind. *Passages in Modern Sculpture*, Cambridge, MA: MIT Press, 1977.

Le Rose, Lauren. "Dutch Design Guru's Viktor and Rolf Bring Their 'Dolls' Collection to the Royal Ontario Museum for Luminato," Style, *National Post*, April 9, 2013, http://news.nationalpost.com/life/dutch-design-gurus-viktor-rolf-bring-their-dolls-collection-to-the-royal-ontario-museum-for-luminato. Assessed November 18, 2015.

Lighthall, Sara. "Why Food Is Less about the Tag and More about the Experience," https://relate.zendesk.com/articles/foodporn-less-about-tag-more-about-experience/. Accessed February 23, 2018.

Lorca, Frederico Garcia. *Theory and Play of the Duende*, trans. A. S. Kline, 2007, http://www.poetryintranslation.com/PITBR/Spanish/LorcaDuende.php. Accessed January 14, 2018.

Mead, Rebecca. "Iris Van Herpen's High Tech Couture," *The New Yorker,* https://www.newyorker.com/magazine/2017/09/25/iris-van-herpens-hi-tech-couture, Accessed July 10, 2018.

Medina, Marcy. "Hermes Opens Final 'Hermesmatic' Pop-Up at Westfield Century City," http://wwd.com/fashion-news/fashion-scoops/hermes-opens-final-hermesmatic-pop-up-at-westfield-century-city-11048056/. Accessed November 24, 2018.

Menkes, Suzy. "Galliano's Diorient Express Runs Out of Steam," *The New York Times*, http://www.nytimes.com/1998/07/21/style/gallianos-diorient-express-runs-out-of-steam.html. Accessed November 28, 2017.

Meyers, William H. "Maxim's Is the Name of the Game," *The New York Times*, http://www.nytimes.com/1987/05/03/magazine/maxim-s-name-is-the-game.html?pagewanted=all. Accessed February 18, 2018.

Michelson, Annette. "'Where Is Your Rupture?': Mass Culture and the Gesamtkunstwerk," *October*, 56, Spring 1991, 42–63.

Mulvagh, Jasne. "FASHION/Modes of Resistance: In Late 1944, Paris Was Free, but the Fashion Industry Was in Tatters. A unique artistic collaboration helped to re-establish French couture. Its heroes were 70cm tall," *Independent*, July 31, 1994, http://www.independent.co.uk/arts-entertainment/fashion-modes-of-resistance-in-late-1944-paris-was-free-but-the-fashion-industry-was-in-tatters-a-1418052.html

Nietzsche, Friedrich. *Jenseits von Gut und Böse*, in *Werke*, Salzburg: Verlag Das Bergland-Buch, v. 4, 1985.

Patton, Elizabeth and Vanessa Friedman. "Collette Fashion Destination Paris Is to Close in December," July 12, 2017, Fashion and Style, *The New York Times*, https://www.nytimes.com/2017/07/12/fashion/colette-paris-sarah-andelman.html. Accessed January 21, 2018.

Poiret, Paul. *En habillant l'epoque*, Paris: Grasset, 1930.

Pollock, Griselda. *Vision and Difference: Feminism, Femininity and Histories of Art*, London and New York: Routledge, 2003.

Prial, Frank J. "Maxim's the Paris Restaurant Is Sold to Cardin Enterprises," *The New York Times*, http://www.nytimes.com/1981/05/06/garden/maxim-s-the-paris-restaurant-is-sold-to-cardin-enterprises.html. Accessed February 16, 2018.

Prose, Francine. "Elsa Schiaparelli: Le Shocking!," *Aperture* 176, Fall 2004, 42–7.

Rehn Wolfman, Ursula. "Richard Wagner's Concept of the '*Gesamtkunstwerk*'", *Interlude*, March 12, 2013, http://www.interlude.hk/front/richard-wagners-concept-of-the-gesamtkunstwerk/

Riewoldt, Otto. *Retail Design*, New York: Nte Neues, 2000.

Riewoldt, Otto, ed. *Brandscaping: Worlds of Experience in Retail Design*, Boston and Berlin: Berhauser Verlag AG, 2002.

Roberts, Mary Louise. "Samson and Delilah Revisited: The Politics of Women's Fashion in 1920s France," *The American Historical Review*, 98(3), June 1993, 657–84.

Rose, Julian. "Objects in the Cluttered Field," *October* 140, Spring 2012, 126.

Rubenstein, Helena. *My Life for Beauty*, New York: Simon and Schuster, 1966.

Safer, Samantha. "Designing Lucile Ltd: Couture and the Modern Interior 1900–1920s," *Journal of the Decorative Arts Society 1850–the Present*, 33, 2009, 38–53.

Sagansky, Gillian. "Capturing the Elusive Givenchy Spring 2016 Show," *W Magazine* online, https://www.wmagazine.com/story/givenchy-spring-2016-marco-brambilla. Accessed December 10, 2017.

Said, Edward W. *Orientalism: Western Conceptions of the Orient.* London: Penguin, 1978, 36.

Savage, John. *The Creation of Youth Culture*, Harmondsworth: Penguin, 2007.

Schmidt, Wolf Gerhard. "Was ist ein '*Gesamtkunstwerk*'? Zur medienhistorischen Neubestimmung des Begriffs," *Arvhiv für Musikwissenschaft*, 68(2), 2011, 157–79.

Secrest, Meryle. *Elsa Schiaparelli*, New York: Knopf, 2014.

Seely, Stephen. "How Do You Dress a Body without Organs? Affective Fashion and Nonhuman Becoming," *Women's Studies Quarterly*, 41(2), Spring/Summer, 2012, 247–65.

Sparke, Penny. "The 'Ideal' and the 'Real' Interior in Elsie de Wolf's 'The House in Good Taste' of 1913," *Journal of Design History*, 16(1), 2003, 63–76.

Specter, Michael. "Le Freak C'est Chic," *The Guardian,* https://www.theguardian.com/theobserver/2003/nov/30/features.magazine47. Accessed November 23, 2017.

Stafford, Jerry. "Presenting Gareth Pugh's Vision for Spring/Summer 2018," *Vogue*, http://www.vogue.co.uk/article/gareth-pughs-springsummer-2018-film. Accessed January 8, 2018.

Steele, Valerie. *The Berg Companion to Fashion*, Oxford: Berg, 2010.

Tindle, Hannah. "Nick Knight and Gareth Pugh on the Future of Fashion," *Dazed*, http://www.dazeddigital.com/fashion/article/37426/1/gareth-pugh-and-nick-knight-on-the-future-of-fashion-film-ss18. Accessed January 6, 2018.

Trahndorff, Karl Friedrich Eusebius. *Ästhetik oder Lehre von Weltanschauung und Kunst*, 2 vols, Berlin, 1827.

Trotter, Cate. "50 Most Beautiful Concept Stores in the World," https://www.linkedin.com/pulse/50-most-beautiful-concept-stores-world-cate-trotter/. Accessed January 15, 2018.

Vreeland, Diana. *D.V.*, Weidenfeld and Nicolson: London, 1984.

Wagner, Richard. *Sämtliche Schriften und Dichtungen*, Leipzig: Breitkopf & Härtel, 12 vols, 1848–1926.

Westwood, Vivienne and Ian Kelly. *Vivienne Westwood*, London: Picador, 2014.

Wilde, Oscar. "The Decay of Dying," in H. Adams, ed., *Critical Theory since Plato*. New York: Harcourt Brace, 1992.

Williams, Geoff. "How Millenials Will Shape Food in 2017," https://www.forbes.com/sites/geoffwilliams/2016/12/31/how-millennials-will-shape-food-in-2017/#5cd004e26a6d. Accessed February 22, 2018.

Wissinger, Elizabeth. *This Year's Model: Fashion, Media, and the Making of Glamour*, New York: New York University Press, 2015.

Wollen, Peter. "Fashion/Orientalism/The Body," *New Formations*, 1, Spring 1987, 5–33.

Wosk, Julie. *Female Robots, Androids, and Other Artificial Eves*, New Brunswick: Rutgers University Press, 2015.

Filmography

The Hunger, dir. Tony Scott, Metro-Goldwyn-Mayer, 1983.

Internet sources not cited above

http://bombmagazine.org/article/2606/santiago-sierra
The Padstow Obby Oss, https://padstowobbyoss.wordpress.com/about/. Accessed January 10,
    2018.
Gareth Pugh, Spring/Summer 2015, Showstudio. https://www.youtube.com/
    watch?v=qeaXJhQyjAI https://www.centrepompidou.fr/cpv/resource/cLjdb4/rjAaKR
https://thecharnelhouse.org/2014/03/01/el-lissitzkys-soviet-pavilion-at-the-pressa-exhibition-in-
    cologne-1928/
http://www.indexmagazine.com/interviews/viktor_and_rolf.shtml
http://www.musee-orangerie.fr/en/article/history-water-lilies-cycle
http://the-widows-of-culloden.tumblr.com/post/58537891727/alexander-mcqueen-ss-1997-la-
    poupee-the.
https://www.ranker.com/list/best-luxury-fashion-brands/ranker-shopping. Accessed February 1,
    2018.
The "Water-Dress". Biomimicry by Iris Van Herpen, Promystyl Blog, International Style and Trend
    Office, http://www.promostyl.com/blog/en/the-water-dress-by-iris-van-herpen/, accessed July
    10, 2018.

www.ingramcontent.com/pod-product-compliance
Ingram Content Group UK Ltd.
Pitfield, Milton Keynes, MK11 3LW, UK
UKHW052006180226
468167UK00007B/315